The Hertfordshire Way

CAMBRIDGESHIRE

ESSEX

LONDON

KEY

Complete walk route ....
Leg starting points e.g. 1. Royston

This book is dedicated to all those persons, known and unknown, who over the years have fought the good fight to protect and open up the footpath network in Hertfordshire. The paths that most of us take for granted would not be so freely accessible but for this band of dedicated walkers who took on vested interests and won for us an excellent system of pathways. May we in turn expand the network of footpaths and protect them for future generations.

Walk not in vain
But with hope.
Hope that you will come again.
Or that others will walk this way
And share your joys.

THE HERTFORDSHIRE WAY

A walker's guide book

Edited by

BERT RICHARDSON

Produced by

The Friends of the Hertfordshire Way

Published by

Castlemead
PUBLICATIONS
WARE

First Published July 1998

CASTLEMEAD PUBLICATIONS
Raynham House, Broadmeads
Ware
Herts SG12 9HY

Proprietors:
WARD'S PUBLISHING SERVICES

ISBN 0 948555 41 6

British Library Cataloguing in Publication Data
A catalogue record for this book is available from the
British Library

Printed and bound in Great Britain by
The Burlington Press (Cambridge) Ltd

Guide to the Hertfordshire Way

Total mileage 166

St Albans Abbey © **Anthony Mackay**

How The Walk Originated

In 1994 the Ramblers' Association made plans to celebrate its 60 year fight to protect our national network of rights of way. Each area of the association was to plan its own celebration. The Hertfordshire and North Middlesex Area decided to do a long distance walk around the county. This was planned and walked by a group of walkers. It was divided into 12 legs and in 1995, the Jubilee Year, over 60 people completed the walk. When it was finished a group remained interested in the route, and with the help of the local area of the RA a committee was formed and the route was expanded to 166 miles in 14 legs. Twelve people started to survey the route and to write guides for each leg. These were checked in the field by other volunteers and the whole work was brought together to form this guide book. When you read it you will notice different styles of writing from each of the contributors. The background research in each leg was provided by the person(s) developing that section of the walk, with additional material (in some places) by Bert Richardson.

A list of contributors:

David Allard Leg 14	Michael Blackman Leg 6
Joyce & George Faldo Leg 4	Sue & Peter Garside Legs 7, 8
Hywel Morris Leg 9	Chris Pagan Leg 12
Bert Richardson Legs 1, 2, 3, 5	Nancy & Michael Scott Legs 10, 11
Roy Wheeler Leg 13	All maps drawn by Colin 'Inky' Hills

The group is now independent but notes its gratitude to Hertfordshire and North Middlesex Area for its support in the early days. The group is now called **Friends of the Hertfordshire Way.**

The distinctive waymarking (costing nearly £4000) of the route has been made possible by the generosity of business firms, local ramblers groups, Watling Chase Community Forest and our own membership. If you would like to join us, and support our aims, details can be found at the back of this guide book.

The Hertfordshire Way

(Hertfordshire Long Distance Walk)

Introduction

The 166 mile trail covers a large part of this beautiful, populous and rich county, (incidentally one of the smallest counties in England, only 634 square miles). It is a county of rich contrasts. In the north east there are wide open panoramas over low hills and rich farm lands as seen in the area around Barkway. Standing on Therfield Heath you can look down on to the flat plains of Cambridgeshire. Then you can enter the steep wooded escarpments of the Chilterns, visit the many ancient and fine market towns, or the Cathedral City of St Albans and the countless picture postcard villages nestling in an intimate landscape of farmland and woods.

To the south of our county is the beginning of the vast spread of London which has swallowed up towns and villages, even counties. Where now is Middlesex except in the name of cricket and other organisations remembering its illustrious past?

In 1801 Hertfordshire had a population of about 100,000 now it is just over the one million mark (1,015,000-1996). It has never been a heavy industrial area but it has seen its own industrial changes from brewing, plaiting of straw, for hats etc. paper making, industries associated with wool such as fulling (cleaning the woven cloth) and silk mills. Today technical industries and service industries dominate the industrial scene.

A good introduction to the county, and how it developed from pre-history, can be found in ëThe Hertfordshire Landscape' by Lionel M Munby, part of the 'Making of The English Landscape' series. (Hodder and Stoughton ISBN 0-340-04459-4, but out of print at this time, although copies are held by Hertfordshire Library Services).

People have settled the area since prehistoric times. On Therfield Heath (see Leg 1) there is a long barrow of the Neolithic Age (2500 BC) and round barrows of the Bronze Age (1000 BC). There is evidence of the Beaker People in Hertfordshire and the ancient Icknield Way, with its associated hill forts, crosses the northern edge of the county. The Iron Age settlers were rudely interrupted, at the height of their power, by the Roman invasion. Many Roman Roads go through Hertfordshire e.g. Ermine Street and Watling Street and our walk crosses the remains of the Roman town, Verulamium, (St Albans).

Hertfordshire was part of the shifting boundary in the Dark Ages between the English settlers (Angles & Saxons) and the later invaders, the Vikings. It was a long and turbulent time before the country became united. A good novel which covers this period is called the 'Conscience of the King' by Alfred Duggan.

In the Medieval period the great abbeys were founded and one can still be seen in St Albans (see Legs 4 & 5). Many fine Medieval churches can be seen on this walk and short detours will be worth your while to seek out some of these (unfortunately due to theft and vandalism some country churches are now locked).

During the 16th to 18th centuries many country estates were established in Hertfordshire e.g. Hatfield House, Knebworth House and Ashridge House. Some of the houses do not survive but our walk will take you through parkland which reminds us of those estates e.g. when you pass through Ayot St Lawrence you will be going through such parkland and Ashridge still has its great house. First a monastery, then a great house, now a management college!

The growth of London and the coming of industry saw some rapid development in the county in the 19th and 20th centuries. An example of this development was the Ovaltine factory at Kings Langley (now owned by the Swiss drug company, Sandoz) with model farms, now sadly gone, to feed its needs (see Legs 7 and 8).

No major rivers flow through the county (the River Lea, a tributary of the Thames is navigable up to Hertford). The Grand Union Canal passes through our county on its way north west (see Leg 7). The railways opened up Hertfordshire for industry and settlement and such towns as Hemel Hempstead and Watford grew from several hundred people to 80,000 plus. Many of the great road routes which fan out from London pass through our county such as the A1, A5, A6, A10 and M1. Finally we saw the first of the Garden Cities (Welwyn Garden City and Letchworth) and the New Towns (Stevenage). The great orbital road the M25 cuts its way through the county (see Legs 7 to 9) not forgetting the electricity pylons, supplying our thirst for power, which you will see as you travel.

Many famous people are associated with Hertfordshire. Samuel Pepys was a regular visitor and once when staying in Baldock he noticed that the landlady was very pretty but '*I durst not take notice of her, her husband being there*'. Queen Elizabeth I, then a princess, was a near prisoner at Hatfield House when the Roman Catholic Queen Mary was on the throne. King James I had a palace at Royston (the start of our walk) from where he hunted on the lands of north Hertfordshire. The so called Rye House Plot to kill King Charles II was hatched on its borders. Isaac Walton of 'Compleat Angler' fame knew the River Lea well. The earliest Christian martyr St Alban was executed in Roman times at the site of the city bearing his name. Francis Bacon lived at Gorhambury (an estate near St Albans through which our walk passes). He is buried in the church of St Michael nearby. Finally George Bernard Shaw made his home in Ayot St Lawrence. His home is now a National Trust property and is close to our route.

In spite of the development most of your walking will be on rural pathways through fields, villages and woods where you can enjoy the peace and forget the might and noise of industry that remind you of the century we live in —— Good walking!

Acknowledgements

We would like to thank the following companies and friends, without whose financial help this project would not have been possible. Almost all of the money donated will be spent to purchase roadside waymarks of the standard set by the Icknield Way signs.

Contributors up to February 1998

*Glaxo Welcome

*Smithkline Beecham

*Cereal Partners UK

*Johnson Matthey

*Members of the society

*Watling Chase Community
  Forest

*Royston & District Group

*Herts & Middlesex Area of the
  R A

*Mid Herts Footpath Society

*East Herts Footpath Society

*Essex & Herts Long Distance
  Walkers

*Donations from friends

We would also wish to thank all the contributors of illustrations in this book. They are Nancy Scott, Bert Richardson, Ted Walsby, David Allard and the Rev. Patrick Bright. Special thanks to Anthony Mackay to reproduce illustrations from his book *Journeys into Hertfordshire* ISBN 0 871199 90 5 and to Tony Rook for permission to reproduce illustrations from his book *A History of Hertfordshire.* ISBN 0 85033 580 9.

We acknowledge a large debt of gratitude to Colin 'Inky' Hills who drew all the maps from rough sketches by Bert Richardson. 'Inky's' work has entailed hours of highly skilled research and mapping which has greatly enhanced this publication.

Travel and Tourist Information

Details of public transport for the County are given in four *Hertfordshire Travel Guides,* covering the Northern, Western, Central and Eastern areas. These guides include all bus, train and London Underground timetables for their respective areas, as well as maps showing bus routes, with detailed street maps of the main town centres. They also have public service operators' addresses and telephone numbers, and some general information such as market days and early closing days. The areas covered are shown in the map below. The guides are available from local Council Offices, libraries and bus stations, or by post from the Passenger Transport Unit, Hertfordshire County Council, P.O. Box 99, Hertford, SG14 2RE. The Passenger Transport Unit also publishes a monthly *Passenger Transport Update* leaflet.

A telephone travel enquiry service is provided by *Hertfordshire Traveline,* between the hours of 0830 and 1730, Mondays to Fridays. From anywhere in the County, a call on 0345 244344 is charged at local rates.

A useful leaflet, *'Bedfordshire, Hertfordshire & Luton - what to do, where to stay',* published by Bedfordshire, Hertfordshire & Luton Tourism Ltd (tel. 01727 813728), is available from Tourist Information Offices in the County. It includes brief notes on the major towns and cities, historical sites, museums, wildlife centres, gardens, canals, rivers, parks, walks and nature trails, entertainment and leisure centres, some hotels and B&B, a map of the county and a summary of main rail services.

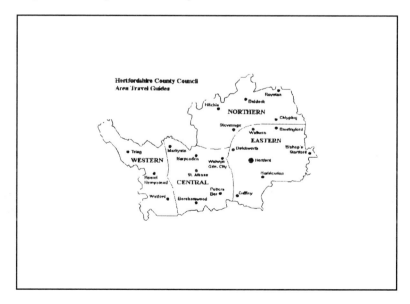

	address	telephone	closed
Baldock Visitor Information Point	The Library, Simpson Drive, Baldock, SG7 6DH	01462 893297	Thur Sun
Berkhamsted Visitor Information Point	The Library, Kings Road, Berkhamsted, HP4 3BD	01442 877638	Wed Sun
Bishop's Stortford Tourist Information Centre	The Old Monastery, Windhill, Bishop's Stortford, CM23 2ND	01279 655831	Sun
Borehamwood Tourist Information Point	Central Reception, Civic Offices, Elstree Way, Borehamwood, WD6 1WA	0181 2077496	Sat Sun
Buntingford Visitor Information Point	The Manor House, High Street, Buntingford	01763 272689	Sat Sun
Dacorum Information Centre	Marlowes, Hemel Hempstead, HP1 1DT	01442 234222	Sun
Hertford Tourist Information Centre	10 Market Place, Hertford, SG14 1DG	01992 584322	Sun *
Hitchin Visitor Information Point	The Library, Paynes Park, Hitchin, SG5 1EW	01462 434738 01462 450133	Wed Sun
Hoddesdon Visitor Information Point	Hoddesdon Library, 98a, High Street, Hoddesdon, EN11 8HD	01992 462296	Thur Sun
Letchworth Tourist Information Point	The Letchworth Shop, 63a, Leys Avenue, Letchworth, SG6 3EU	01462 487868	Wed Sun

	address	telephone	closed
Rickmansworth Information Point	Three Rivers House, Northway, Rickmansworth, WD3 1RL	01763 243292	Sat Sun
Royston Visitor Information Point	The Library, Market Hill, Royston, SG8 9JN	01279 655831	Thur Sun
South Mimms Tourist Information Centre	M25 Service Area, Bignells Corner, Potters Bar, EN6 3QQ	01707 643233	
St Albans Tourist Information Centre	The Town Hall, Market Place, St Albans, AL3 5DJ	01727 864511	Sun†
Stevenage Visitor Information Point	Central Library, Southgate, Stevenage, SG1 1HD	01438 369441	Sun
Tring Information Centre	99 Akeman Street, Tring, HP23 6AA	01442 823347	Sun
Welwyn Garden City Leisure Information Centre	Campus West, The Campus, Welwyn Garden City, AL8 6BX	01707 390653	Sun

* Open Sunday afternoons, first Sunday in the month from May to September.

† Open Sundays (10.30 am to 4.30 p.m.), mid-July to mid-September.

The Walk

On this walk there are many fine villages, historic towns and other interesting tourist sites. For example; the remains of the Roman city (Verulamium) at St Albans, Letchworth the first planned garden city and the beautiful Ashridge Estate (NT). There is also a fine selection of public houses for lunch time refreshment. Almost all the walk is on public rights of way, (there are a few sections on permissive paths, but they are clearly noted in the text). Hertfordshire is one of the more enlightened counties concerning public rights of way and most are clearly marked. The main problem is the non-reinstatement of cross field paths after ploughing or cropping or allowing crops to grow on them. The second major problem is the ploughing up of paths on the edges of fields. **Both these practices are illegal and should be reported.** If you find these problems, or any other, on your walk please write to *Hertfordshire County Council, Environmental Management Department, Rights of Way, County Hall, Hertford. SG13 8DN.* State the date of your observations, what the problem is, and the place and grid reference, if possible.

Public Rights of Way

Please note that public rights of way are the Queen's Highway and you have a legal right to be on them at any time. They have a legal status. It is important to remember that many people, over the years, have campaigned to open these paths to the public, the main campaigner being the Ramblers' Association. Membership of this group is recommended; it provides four magazines a year and a book full of useful and important information including many pages of bed and breakfast accommodation in Britain. You can also become a member of a local walking group.

The address is:

> *The Ramblers' Association,*
> *1/5 Wandsworth Road,*
> *LONDON,*
> *SW8 2XX*

Safety and other matters in your planning

Safety is important at all times around farm machinery and industrial sites but two areas of safety are very important; **roads and railway lines.** Even the narrow roads which we will cross and walk along, at times, can carry fast moving traffic, so be vigilant and obey the rules of safety. If you are walking in a party make sure the whole group is made aware of your approach to roads. Occasionally it is necessary to cross main line railways; do this with extreme care. **Clothing.** This is lowland Britain and the most important item is footwear. Strong boots or wellingtons and thick socks are recommended. Hertfordshire is a county of clay and it can be very muddy. Always carry waterproofs in Britain!

The route
The route is meant to be followed by reading the detailed text. The maps at the beginning of each leg are for information as to direction and places and not for detailed route guidance. They will be useful for reference to Ordnance Survey maps. Small sketch maps are included within the text to help at slightly more complicated spots. **To help you to follow the route it has been waymarked at nearly all road crossings with its own distinctive sign.**

Added information in the text
In addition to the maps and the detailed walking text there is background information which is provided for those not familiar with the area and which we hope will increase your enjoyment as you travel through this beautiful county.

Respect for the countryside
Hertfordshire is a farming county so please close and fasten all gates **you have opened** and dogs must be kept on leads among stock and close to woodland where game birds could be nesting. Please do not leave any rubbish; take it home with you.

Cars
If you are using your car please park it with due consideration for landowners and residents in the area. Do remember on Sundays not to use church parking spaces.

Waymarks on the route
Where the route crosses a road, in nearly all cases, there is a distinctive **Hertfordshire Way sign.** We hope, when funds become available, to waymark the route on the paths making it even more visible on the ground.

Maps
Pathfinder Maps (PFM) have all public footpaths marked clearly and are easy to follow with a little experience and at about £4 each are good value.

Important notice. The Pathfinder series is gradually being withdrawn and replaced by the **Explorer Maps (EGM).** They are to the same scale as the Pathfinder series but will cover a larger area. At this point there is only one in this area (round Tring and the Chilterns). In future editions of this guide book we will make more reference to this series instead of the Pathfinder Maps. **As they are published they will replace the Pathfinder and our references to map numbers, at the start of each walk, will no longer be correct.** Ordnance Survey has not produced a guide to map sheet numbers for this series or the exact publication dates (earliest 1999) so we cannot give any more information at this time.

Landranger (LRM) these maps cover a larger area than the above maps and are good for general directions but are more difficult to follow when walking as their scale is smaller.

Great care has been taken to ensure that the descriptions of the route are as accurate as is possible but various factors affect the printed word and an individual's interpretation of the written word does vary! Also features on the land can change, for example houses can be built on fields after the description has been written.

Key to Maps in This Guide

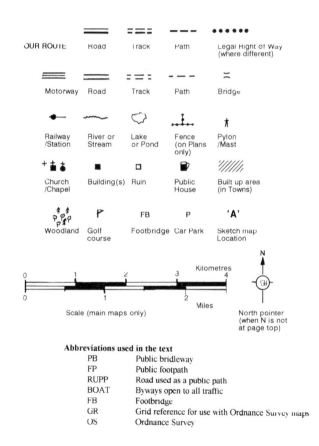

Abbreviations used in the text

PB	Public bridleway
FP	Public footpath
RUPP	Road used as a public path
BOAT	Byways open to all traffic
FB	Footbridge
GR	Grid reference for use with Ordnance Survey maps
OS	Ordnance Survey

Leg 1:   Royston to Wallington

Length   10¹/₂ miles
Start   The Cross, Royston **GR** 356407
Finish   Wallington **GR** 293338
Maps   **PFM** 1026 & 1049 **LRM** 153, 154, 166
Public Transport: Royston has regular bus and train
             services with major centres. Wallington has no
             service to speak of but is only 3¹/₂ miles from Baldock
             which has trains and buses
Pubs   Therfield 4 miles, Sandon 7 miles

The Route. This is the most dramatic leg from the scenery point of view with the first half of the walk climbing and following the scarp slopes of the chalk hills. Once on the top we come into a gentle rural landscape of fields and hedgerows with gently rolling hills, so typical of Hertfordshire. On the Heath there is a long barrow and several round barrows (see introduction). In spring, on the old chalk grassland, you will see a wide range of wild flowers.

We are starting in the north of the county in Royston, a busy, small market town. It has a range of industries including Johnson Matthey, who include gold refining among their many skills. Historically it grew up where an old Roman road crosses the prehistoric Icknield Way. It was not a Saxon parish but grew around a Priory established by the Normans. The Icknield Way long distance path passes through the town. Royston has a market on Wednesday and Saturday, a library, a museum and an ample supply of public houses. It has a unique cave, cut into the chalk in medieval times, with interesting carvings in the chalk. The Parish Church is part of the old priory with a Victorian chancel, and is worth a visit. Royston was the centre from where King James I hunted on the open chalk downlands. There is very little of his palace remaining. Therfield Heath on the edge of the town is a small remnant of that vast hunting ground. A very good guide to the town can be obtained from the library.

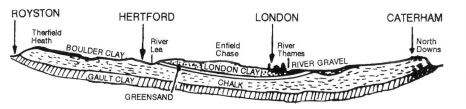

Diagram 1. The town is built at the base of the chalk hills. This scarp slope of chalk slowly dips under the London Basin to re-appear as the North Downs, south of London. On the top of the scarp the chalk is covered with boulder clay (that is why the footpaths in the county are sometimes sticky in winter) deposited in the last Ice Age.

19

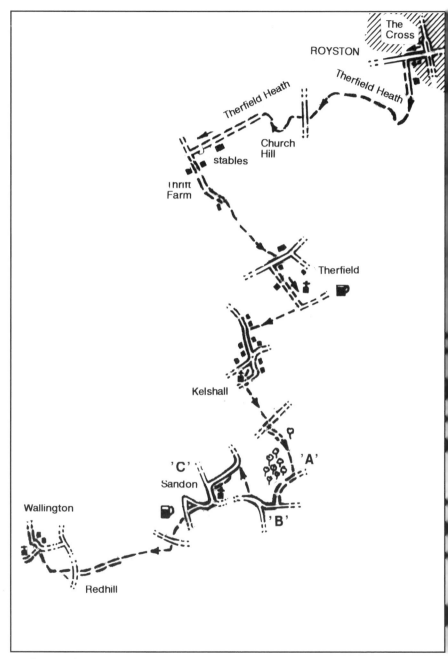

Route map for Leg 1

If you are staying in Royston there are lots of places to visit in the area. Cambridge is only a few miles away, as is the fine National Trust property of Wimpole Hall and the Imperial War Museum site at Duxford with its magnificent collection of aircraft.

The Walk

1. Leave The Cross travelling west along the Baldock Road and look out for the golf club house at the beginning of the Heath. Turn sharp left in front of this building on to the Heath, keeping a straight line to a hill on the horizon. When you reach its summit there is a small plantation of immature trees. Follow the track to the right of them and circle the valley on a clear track (farm land should always be on your left until you reach a road). This route round the south side of the Heath is partly open heathland and partly woodland and it is 1½ miles to the road. You cannot go wrong if you keep farm land always on your left! Before the road you will have a golf course on your right. *This golf course is on common land and you have a right to cross it if you wish. There are several barrows on the Heath if you wish to explore.*

2. Cross the road into trees, follow the track to some large beech trees and turn left. Now take a diagonal route through these open trees, largely clear of undergrowth, to come out on to open ground. You want the top of the last hill on your left. It forms a fairly steep ridge on both sides.

Royston Parish Church in winter

© Rev. P Bright

2. The steep drop to your left will have a flat, slightly wide, dry valley if you are on the correct hill! Walk along its crest and drop to a chain stile, go through it and turn right along a track until you come to a tall thick tree hedge on your left. You follow this hedge keeping it on your immediate left. **Be careful here that you have not gone into a field with a hedge on both sides!** You should have the open heath on your right with the A505 below you. Keep walking along this hedge until you come to the western end of the Heath and a farm road into Thrift Farm on your left. You will have passed the racing stables about 200 yards before this point, through the hedge on your left; this is not Thrift Farm.

3. Turn left into the farmyard and walk between the farm buildings on each side. Continue straight on along the farm track past a rifle range on your right on the site of an old farm. You will now have a hedge on your left, follow it to a guide post. You now leave the hedge and go slightly right, crossing an open field towards a hedge and trees; here you will find another guide post. Keep this hedge to your right and soon enter a gully deep in trees (it can be wet here in winter). You climb this gully until you come out to a road on the edge of Therfield.

If you want to explore this village and visit the pub, turn left then right. There are many fine houses in the village though the church was completely rebuilt in Victorian times. Allow about œ of an hour, excluding pub visit!

4. To restart the route comes back to this spot. From where we emerged on to the road, turn right and look for a footpath sign pointing to your left. Take this path and after a short distance there is a water tower on your right.

Pause about here for a while and look to your left to see a beautiful old manor house called Tuthill Manor. This was a cow shed until it was discovered fairly recently and fully restored to its former glory.

5. Continue until you meet a T junction and turn right on to the path until you meet a road on the edge of Kelshall. Turn left on to this road and walk through the pretty village. Ignore the road on your left with a small roundabout but soon your road turns right, go straight on to the cul de sac. After 50 yards look for a footpath on your right and follow this into a churchyard. In the churchyard is a much damaged base of a fifteenth century cross. You need to go out through the main gate but you can take time to explore the church.   Cross the road and go through the gate opposite looking for a stile on your right in a wooden fence. Climb the stile, turn left and follow the fence to its end. Keeping your direction drop gently as you cross a field to a hedge. Go through this hedge and gently climb to cross a small section of field to another hedge/ditch.   Keep this on your right.   You will now drop to a wide farm track making a T junction to your path.

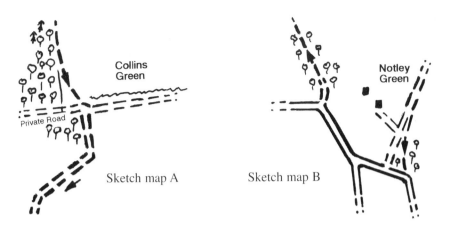

Collins Green

Private Road

Sketch map A

Notley Green

Sketch map B

6. Turn right onto this and follow it for about 200 yards and take the next track on your left. You pass a wood on your left and then join a wood on your right. At the end of the wood the route is a bit complicated *so consult map A*. Keep on this bridleway until you reach the road *then follow the instructions on map B.*

Kelshall Church in winter   © Bert Richardson

23

7. After leaving the road, as shown on map B, you will now be on a bridleway with trees on both sides. You will reach a road on a sharp corner, turn left on to this road keeping an eye out for a footpath on your left. Take this path and you will come out in Sandon Churchyard (the church is worth a visit). *Map C will show you the way through the village. The village, at the time of writing, still has a shop so help to keep it open by buying some refreshments.*

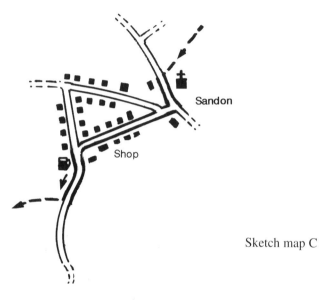

Sketch map C

8. Your footpath is just after an excellent pub on the same side. Follow this path through several fields (in the second field keep about 10 yards from the hedge on your left) before emerging onto a wide green with a road running through the centre. Cross the road to a gravel drive. Walk up this drive and look for a narrow footpath on your right leading to a field. Cross this field and come to a farm track. Turn right and follow it for about a mile to a road with a house on your left (part of Redhill). Cross the road to a footpath that, at first, drops to a shallow ditch, then follows a hedge climbing steadily. You will reach a junction of footpaths, take the second one on your right which is a crossfield path with a farm on your left. Once you reach the road you are in the village of Wallington and you have finished the first leg of this Long Distance Path!

Researched and walked by Bert Richardson

Leg 2: Wallington to Willian (Letchworth)

Length 12 miles
Start Car Park Wallington **GR** 293338
Finish Willian **GR** 223306
Maps **PFM** 1049 & 1073 **LRM** 166
Public Transport Wallington (see Leg 1). Willian has only a local bus service but is only 1½ miles from Letchworth with main line trains and buses.
Pubs Weston 6 miles (several to choose from)

The Route. It is similar to the first leg but we get our first brief glimpse of urban settlement as we pass within a few miles of Stevenage, go under the A1(M) and finish on the edge of Letchworth.

The Walk
1.There is a small car park in Wallington, *see Sketch map A.* From the car park turn right and go straight on for 50 yards. *As you go along this stretch of road notice a plaque on a cottage on your right to commemorate*

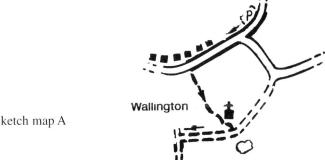

Sketch map A

Wallington

George Orwell who lived here for a period. Then take the footpath on your left which leads you to the church. Go out through the gate (pond opposite) turn right onto a track and follow it as it turns left.

2. After about ¼ mile look out for a waymark on your left and almost immediately following there will be one on your right; take this footpath. Keep a hedge on your right. Soon you will enter a wood, it is well waymarked so you should have no difficulty with your route. On coming out of the wood keep the wood on your left. Soon you will walk between a bank on your right and a hedge on the other side.

3 **Cross the A 507 with great care** and take the footpath, nearly opposite, as shown in Sketch map B (it is not correct as shown on the OS maps). When you come to a road go straight ahead passing Clothall Church on your right.

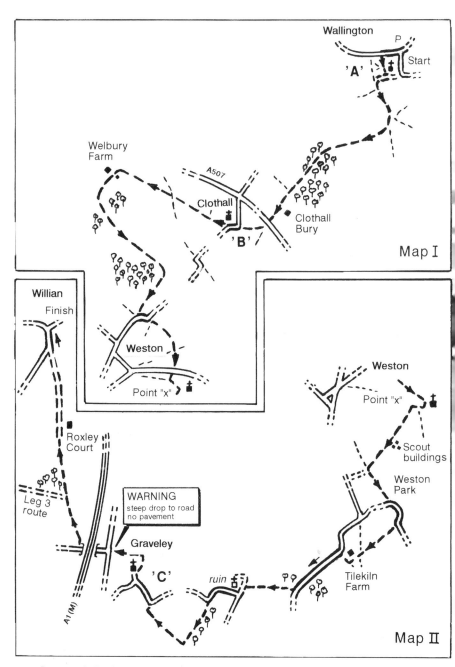

Route map for Leg 2

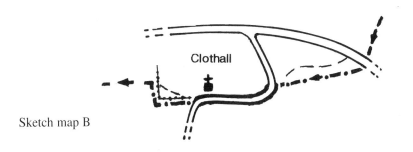

Sketch map B

The church is well worth a visit. It has some fine monumental brasses. One commemorates John Ventner, Rector in 1404, and another to the wife and sixteen children of William Bramfield.

4. When the road suddenly turns left you go straight on *(sketch map B again)* Here the footpath turns slightly right into a field but you go straight on taking a sharp turn right at the end of the fence then a sharp left to regain the line of the path.

5. The A507 can now be seen and heard on your right. Follow this route crossing other paths and keep heading for the farm buildings ahead. When you reach the farm buildings turn left into the farmyard and into a field with a fence on your right. At a gate turn sharp left and climb steeply to a little nick in the ridge. Once over the ridge the hedge will be on your right side, just follow this track round a wood to the road.

6. Cross the road going left and almost immediately on your right is your footpath going down the side of a house and into a field. Keep a straight line crossing the middle of the field. Head for a sharp corner in the hedge, slightly right, where there is a waymark. Look for the stile ahead, cross it, and keeping the right fence in sight, look for a footpath sign in front of a house. Then cross into the road, turn right and look for a footpath on your left going up the drive of a house. Follow this path to a narrow lane, turn left to gain Weston Church.

In the church yard is the famous grave of the giant Jack - o'- Legs. The legend states that he was a robber of travellers and the men of Baldock finally caught him near their town and before they slew him they granted his request that they would bury him where an arrow, which he shot from his bow, fell. The arrow soared three miles to Weston and glanced off the church tower to rest where you now find his giant grave.

7. At the church gate turn right onto another clear path. From this path take the second footpath on your ~~right~~ Left. *(Note if you carry on at this point for 500 yards you come out in the village of Weston with the Red Lion pub in front of you, return to the last spot to continue your walk).* Keep straight along this path, passing some wooden scout huts on your left,

27

Weston, The Red Lion   © Anthony Mackay

then cross a drive and go under a large chestnut tree. Go straight across
this field heading slightly left to a metal fence, follow it until a kissing gate
lets you into a drive, cross it and follow a wood on your left. Look for a
stile near two large trees. Now keep an eye out for other stiles ahead of
you but slightly left, until you finally come out onto a road at a very sharp
corner.

8. Go straight ahead. The road very soon turns sharply right and in the
same distance turns sharply left; at this point go straight on, keeping a
straight line with a fence and trees on your left. You will reach a farm on
your immediate right (Tilekiln Farm). Turn right after you have passed

the last of the farm buildings to the road in front of the farm, turn left onto it.

9. Following the road, a wood will appear on your left. Where a wood starts on your right look out for double gates and a footpath sign. Turn right at this sign and follow this track until you come out onto a road with a ruined church opposite.

This is the Church of St Etheldreda and was the centre of the village of Chesfield. It is one of the many deserted villages. This village is now only represented by a farm and a few scattered houses. You can view the ruin.

10. At this point turn left and in a hundred yards, at a T junction, turn right with the ruin on your right. Follow this road, there is a sharp left bend and then a sharp right bend. At this second bend leave the road and go straight on. As you follow this track you can see pylons ahead and beyond them the large building in the distance is the Lister Hospital in the town of Stevenage.

Stevenage is one of the new towns circling London, which were set up after the Second World War. It is still expanding with a wide range of industry stretching along the A1(M) Corridor. It has an extensive modern, if cold looking, shopping centre with ample parking.

11. Before you reach the pylons look for a signpost pointing right. Take this footpath through the middle of a large field with the pylons dropping away to your left. When you come to a hedge keep it on your right (waymarked). Keep straight on until you reach a large hedge across your

Ruins of Chesfield Church   © Bert Richardson

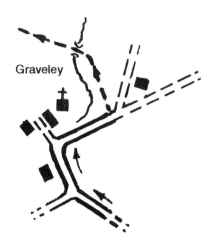

Graveley

Sketch map C

path, turn right along it (waymarked), keeping straight on until you turn left onto the road. When this road turns left take the road opposite and make for Graveley Church. *At this point consult map C.*

Graveley Church and the nearby 17th century Graveley Hall and Church Manor are well worth a look or even a camera snap.

12. As you pass the church (on your left) the farm track branches into two, take the left one but immediately take a footpath on your left. When you come to a bridge over a small ditch on your left, cross it and follow a

Gravely Church

© Ted Walsby

hedge on your left, steadily climbing. Keep straight on through a fruit farm with the noise of the A1(M) traffic ahead of you. At some hedges you will begin to drop to the old A1. **Take great care here for you drop suddenly down a steep bank and there is no footpath!** Take the road opposite and go under the A1(M) turning immediately right onto a gravel track. Follow this all the way to Willian (about 1½ miles), passing Roxley Court on your right. Once in Willian you have reached the end of Leg 2 and you are 1½ miles from the centre of Letchworth.

Willian is now part of Letchworth Garden City but still keeps lots of its charm. The church is well worth a visit. There are some fine gems of medieval work. Part of a Tudor screen is left in the chancel arch. There are also some monuments in the church including the figures of Edward Lacon with his wife and three children.

Letchworth is the world's first garden city. It was conceived by Ebenezer Howard in 1903. It incorporates fine avenues of trees and a pleasant mixed style of domestic architecture and is worth a visit if this is your first time in Hertfordshire.

Researched and walked by Bert Richardson

Leg 3: Willian (Letchworth) to Codicote

Length 12 miles
Start Willian **GR** 223306
Finish Codicote **GR** 214186
Maps **PFM** 1049, 1072, 1073, 1095, 1096 **LRM** 166
Public Transport Letchworth (see Leg 2). Codicote has
local buses connecting with surrounding towns.
Pubs All villages we pass through have pubs and there is
one in the country at **GR** 198254.

The Route. This is an excellent scenic leg with some fine villages and
farm land. It is also a well wooded route with areas of parkland. It has
some outstanding view points on a clear day so be on the look out and not
just mile crunching!

The Walk
1. Proceed *as shown in map A* and follow the road to Roxley Court. At
the house go straight on, you will come to a plantation of trees on your
right. Turn right at the end of the trees through a bar gate (this is not a

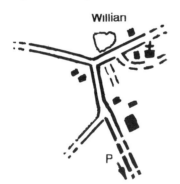

Sketch map A

right of way but a permissive path shown on the OS map as a track).
When you gain the road turn left, **take great care as the road is narrow
and there is no footpath.** Coming into Great Wymondley look for the
Green Man pub on your right. Opposite it is a footpath, take it to the
church (keep to the left of a garage up a narrow path).

*A lot of research has been done on the archaeology of the village where a Roman
villa and cemetery have been discovered. Near to the church there are outlines of
two fields which are of a size that was allocated to retired Roman army veterans
(when they retired they had a right to a certain area of land in the conquered
territories). The church has some Norman features. Not on the route but just
outside the village stands Delamere House a red-bricked Tudor building, once the
property and residence of Cardinal Wolsey. On his death bed, after his fall from
grace with Henry VIII, he said 'Had I but served God as diligently as I have*

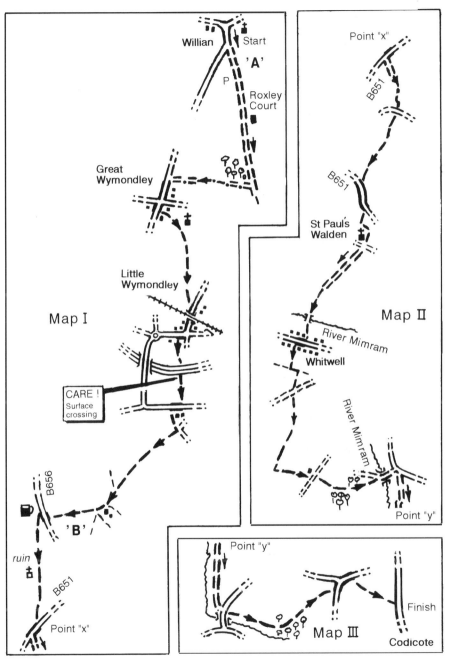

Route map for Leg 3

Based upon Ordnance Survey map with permission.
Crown copyright reserved

One of the restored carvings on
Willian Church tower
© Bert Richardson

served the King, He would not have given me over in my grey hairs' (1530). On the walk, just after we leave the church on our left is the site of a medieval castle. A little further on the walk is the village of Little Wymondley which has a fine 17th century timber framed hall with a fine cluster of chimneys.

2. Cross the churchyard, and close to a roofed gate, take the footpath ahead across a large field travelling diagonally to the left. Find a pond in the hedge and go to the left of it into another field. Cross the next two fields, keeping your direction ahead, to a gate and farm buildings on the opposite side of the road. Turn right on to the road and go under the railway. You are now in the village of Little Wymondley. At the crossroads turn right and almost immediately turn left onto a footpath before the Buck's Head pub.

Before you enter this path be warned that there is a fast dual carriageway to cross. If you have any doubts about your ability to cross this road take a 1 mile detour as follows (all road walking). Carry on along the road past the pub until you come to a crossroads, turn left and follow this road to the next junction. Turn left again into Titmore Green and when you reach the pub the Hermit of Redcoates on your left you are back on track.

3. If you are not taking the detour follow the footpath and come to a water tower on your left. Soon you will begin to drop to the dual carriageway **(cross with extreme care! and complain to your MP and the Ministry of Transport that a footbridge is urgently needed).** Carry straight on and on reaching the road turn right, and opposite the Hermit of Redcoats pub, take the footpath.

4. Cross two fields keeping near to the left hedge, on entering the third field cross to the far hedge and follow it right until you come to a broken stile and a bridge. Cross into a field and immediately out of it and continue along a hedge on your right. When the hedge turns right you carry on across the field heading for a farm on the skyline. As you near a hedge aim for its right corner and within 10 yards of that corner there are steps through the hedge to a fence. Follow this in a straight line, keeping the farm ahead of you, until you reach a farm track which you take to the farm (Almshoe Bury). With a large farm building on your right and the main buildings on your left, go through the farmyard and then behind the building that was on your right (see map B). The farm track crosses your next footpath and it is possible to use this track to point A. The path comes out on to the road opposite the Royal Oak pub.

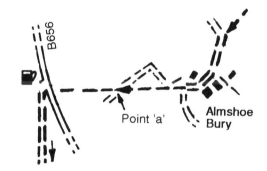

Sketch map B

Point 'a'

Almshoe Bury

5. **Cross the road with care** to the pub and go up a path to the left between the pub and a shed. Follow the line of telegraph posts with a hedge on your immediate left. Climb steadily to the ruin of Minsden Chapel which held its last wedding in 1738. *Go inside and see the gravestone to the historian Reginald Hine. Before you start again stop to see the excellent views.* You will now start to drop steadily on a clear path to a road. Cross, turning right, and within a few yards follow a clear path on your left until you reach a narrow road with houses, keep straight on with houses on both sides. Within a hundred yards leave the road for a footpath straight ahead (go between two stones and over a stile). Keep a hedge on your right, cross another stile and drop down through trees to another road.

6. Cross, and take a stile into a field and follow a clear footpath. When you cross the next stile there will be a wood on your left, keep straight on to the **busy B651, cross with care** and turn left, **this is a dangerous road with no footpath.** Go past the Sue Ryder Home on your left and look for a footpath on the same side and take it. Keep the field edge on your immediate left. On coming to a drive turn left and then right into the churchyard. Cross the churchyard to a road take the track opposite.

Ruins of Minsden Chapel   © Nancy Scott

The church will repay a visit. It has an unusual interior with an English Baroque chancel (the part in front of the altar). It was designed and built in 1727 by Edward Gilbert with a barrel vaulted ceiling and painted plaster walls. The Queen Mother was baptised here in 1900.

7. Shortly, on your left, you will pass a house with ornate windows and very soon, on your right, you will catch glimpses of The Bury, the house where the Queen Mother was born. *The grounds are occasionally open to visitors.* When the track turns right to The Bury carry straight on through a kissing gate. At first keep a hedge on your left and slowly drop to a small river, first crossing a farm road. Cross the river and go into the village of Whitwell.

The village was once part of the more important St Paul's Walden but outgrew its parent though it is still part of the Parish of St Paul's Walden. The High Street is lined with an interesting blend of half timbered Elizabethan houses, brick fronted Georgian houses and Victorian villas. It has two fine pubs and some shops.

8. Turn right into the village and look out for a footpath on your left between buildings, take this footpath. When you come to an open field turn left and almost immediately right alongside three trees. When you have partly crossed the field you will come to a telegraph post and a

left

footpath, turn ~~right~~ on to this path, cross a farm road, climbing a slight rise and drop down to a hedge, cross the stile.

9. Start to climb going slightly right on a clear path. If the farmer has not reinstated the path head towards a telegraph pole on your right but keep about 50 yards from it (look back for some fine views). Over the ridge you drop to a hedge passing between two large trees and turn left on a track towards a barn which you pass on your left. After a house on your left cross a drive and look for a footpath on your immediate left through the gate and across the field and over a stile.

10. Keep a hedge on your right until you cross another stile and the hedge is now on your left. A wood is now on the hedge side and when you reach the end of it cross a stile and drop slightly left to a drive. Turn right onto the drive and go over a ruined bridge. Notice you have been walking in old parkland and below the sad looking bridge is the remains of an ornamental lake.

11. You now meet a road, turn right and almost immediately go off on a track on the ~~left,~~ *right,* keep the small river on your right. On reaching a road

Whitwell, The Bull Inn

© Nancy Scott

37

turn right along it, after about 100 yards turn left on to a bridleway. The river is now below you on the right. You soon come to a wood. On entering the wood (about 30 yards) leave the main track to take a narrow path climbing left into the wood. Keep a look out for some half hidden steps on your left (they come up very soon after taking this path). If you miss them retrace your steps until you find them. At the top of the steps cross a stile and then a second one into an open field. You now cross several fields bearing slightly right all the time, look out for the stiles! The top of a pylon will appear in front of you, keep it to your left as you approach the woods on your right. You enter the woods and quickly drop to a road. *Note that the OS map shows the path coming out at the road junction but it actually comes out south of it.*

12. Turn left to the junction and right at the junction. Keep a look out for a signpost and kissing gate on your right. Take this path in the tree belt until you come to open fields, follow this to a white bungalow (an old gatehouse). Here you come out into Codicote. There is a garden centre about 200 yards to your left which serves teas. Turn right and walk into the centre of the village where there are shops and pubs and where this leg finishes.

Researched and walked by Bert Richardson

Leg 4: Codicote to St. Albans City Railway Station

Length   12 miles
Start   Codicote **GR** 215183
Finish   St. Albans City Railway Station **GR** 155072
Maps   **PFM** 1095, 1096, 1119   **LRM** 166
Public Transport   Codicote (see Leg 3) St Albans: National
    trains & buses
Pubs   Ample on route (see route description)

The Route. We taste a little literature and theatre on part of this walk when we visit the home of George Bernard Shaw. We see parklands and ruined churches on the way, prehistoric sites and finally our first urban walk as we make our way to the centre of the fine town of St Albans - a feast indeed!

The Walk

1. In Codicote High Street, at the traffic lights, take the St Albans Road (the right hand fork). In approximately 250 yards take the footpath on the right. Proceed along the path to wooden steps, cross a track and go down another set of steps to a road. Turn left to Codicote Bottom Farm and left again. In approximately 100 yards take the footpath right by Ayot Lodge. Ahead, left of a field gate, a footpath runs along a fence which leads to the gates of Ayot House, go out of the gates and turn right through Ayot St Lawrence.

In the village there is a lot to see. The house where George Bernard Shaw lived and wrote many of his great plays is now owned by the National Trust and well worth a visit. There is a ruin of the church pulled down by Sir Lionel Lyde to be replaced by a classically styled building in its own park. Ayot House is a Queen Anne style building built on to the basic Tudor manor house where William Parr, brother to Catherine, Henry VIII's queen, lived.

2. Go past the pub on your left and a ruined church on your right taking the footpath by the side of the white cottage (Ruin Cottage). Cross the meadow by the right hand path to the 'new church' *(this was built to fit in with the style of the 'grand' house and is worth a visit).* Go round the right hand side of the church to a drive, turning left with the church on your left. When you come to a road turn right and follow it to the second footpath on the left at a bend in the road.   Follow the main path through an avenue of trees, at a stile bear left on to a long track. In approximately 450 yards on the left hand side go through a self closing gate, onto a path passing in front of the golf club house. Keep bearing left to a track going past the practice range. Along this path, where the path forks, bear right to a gate, exit and walk the path to the road. Cross the road to the path

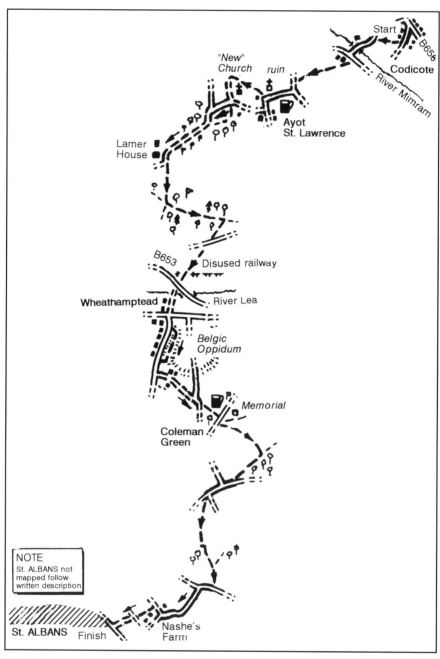

Route map for Leg 4

Based upon Ordnance Survey map with permission.
Crown copyright reserved

The ruined church, Ayot St :Lawrence   © Nancy Scott

opposite, go through iron gates, then follow down the path and under a bridge to a ford. Follow through to a road. The Nelson pub is on the corner. Cross the road to Dyke Lane.

The road runs alongside a great prehistoric earthwork known as Devils Dyke. Look out for a plaque. This earthwork is part of a great Iron Age settlement of the Belgae Tribe (known to the Romans as the Catuvellauni). They ruled large parts of Hertfordshire and were conquered by Julius Caesar when he stormed their capital, Oppidum, in 54 BC This capital has been associated with this structure so you are probably on the site of a great battle fought by the famous Roman General and Emperor.

3. You can walk through the bottom of the dyke but be sure to come back on to the road when you can go no further along the dyke bottom. Follow the road to Beech Hyde Farm, turning left through the farm until you reach a side road where, 40 yards to your right, you take a field path and go through light woods to Coleman Green and the John Bunyan pub.

Nearby is a house chimney stack, just north of the pub, all that is left of a house where, by tradition, John Bunyan is said to have preached and occasionally to have lived. It was demolished in 1877 when a plaque was placed there.

4. At Coleman Green turn right along the lane for some 50 yards to a footpath on the left hand side. There are two paths here; take the right hand one to Titnols Wood. Turn right on to a path on the edge of the

wood to a stile. Cross the stile and proceed towards houses and a road. Turn right down the road to a gravel lane on the left hand side. Immediately take a footpath on the right hand side (by the Hollybush sign). Cross some fields passing on the left hand side of a wooded spring (Harlowdell Spring) and down to Fairfold's Farm.

5. On the road go right and take the left hand lane to Nashe's Farm. Leave the lane on the right hand side just past some hay sheds. Look out for a track on your left and take this to Nashe's Farm. Go down hill to a road, cross into a play area, going forward up to houses, cross the road and go forward coming into Jersey Lane. Turn left along the lane, crossing two roads to emerge at Marshalswick Lane. Cross the road into Marshals Drive.

St Albans Abbey © Tony Rook

6. On the left hand side take a gated path. Going through a small wood keep to the right hand fork. On reaching a road turn right and cross the road and turn left into Woodstock Road North. Turn right at the second road (Brampton Road). At the end of this road cross into York Road. In 50 yards on the left hand side enter the gate of Clarence Park. Bear left following the path round, exit the park on the left hand side and re-enter proceeding on a left hand path and exit from the park by the cafe/restaurant. Turn right and cross the road, take the second turning on the left, which will lead you to St Albans City Railway Station on the right. *(See next leg for instructions to town centre).*

Researched and walked by Joyce and George Faldo

Leg 5: St Albans City Railway Station to Markyate

Length 10$^{1}/_{2}$ miles
Start Railway (City) Station **GR** 155072
Finish Markyate **GR** 062164
Maps **PFM** 1119 & 1095 **LRM** 166
Public Transport St Albans (see Leg 4). Markyate has local
services which include Dunstable and St Albans.
Pubs Redbourn at **GR** 111117 (just off your route) and
in the town. Flamstead also has pubs.

The Route. For those who like history and our English Heritage the start
of this leg is for you. With Medieval splendour, a Roman city to walk on,
and three fine settlements en route. Add to this a small river, water mills
and some fine scenery, and you have it all!

*The town will repay time spent in it, with good shops and lots of history. St Albans
is named after the first British martyr who was executed on the site of the Abbey,
outside the town, by the Roman authorities in A.D.209.   The Roman town
(Verulamium) lies just south of the city. It has a good museum, hypocaust in situ,
a Roman theatre and sections of the city walls. The magnificent Norman and
Medieval Abbey (built largely of bricks taken from the Roman city) is worth a visit.
There are two other museums. Don't forget when you visit the Abbey to put at
least a £1 per person in the box as the building receives no state subsidy and
whatever your religious belief the building needs preserving for future generations to enjoy.*

The Walk

1. As you walk out of the railway station turn right at the road, cross the
rail bridge and you are heading into the city centre. You are in the city
centre when you meet an imposing white building with Greek columns;
turn left, cross the crossroads and look out for the Abbey and head for it.
From the cloisters side of the Abbey go through a public park down to the
little River Ver to an old mill and pub (Fighting Cocks). Cross the river
and keep an eye out for the remains of the Roman city walls (worth
exploring if you have the time). Pass to the left of the lake (the site of a
Roman cemetery) and turn right, heading for the Roman Museum. Next
to the museum is a car park with a church beyond. Follow the boundary
nearest to the church going away from the museum and look for a footpath
into the churchyard, pass the church and come to a main road, cross on
the controlled crossing and go into the gates of the lodge (a notice saying
Roman Theatre). *The next part is a permissive path and not a right of way
and is closed for one day a year. If you are unfortunate enough to choose
this day then go as follows: at the road turn right and right at the
roundabout then walk the unpleasant road to Bow Bridge. (We need a
right of way through this estate, not a permissive path.)*

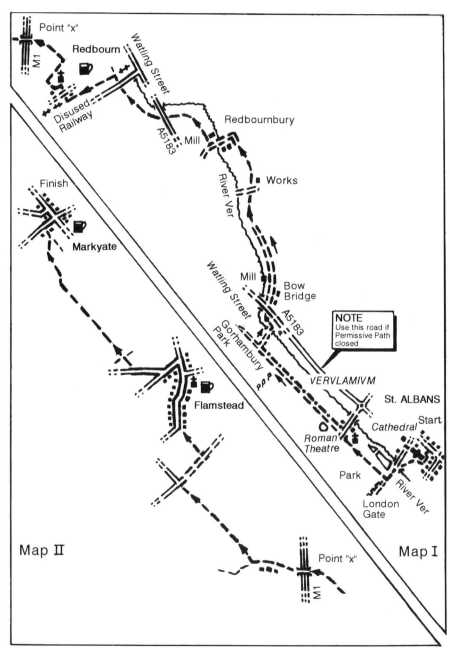

Route map for Leg 5

You are now in the middle of the Roman City with ruins buried beneath your feet! Very little of the town has been excavated so there is still much to learn about this settlement. You are walking approximately along the line of the old main road through the city and the line of trees that crosses the path ahead of you is all that remains of the walls and gates.

2. After ³/₄ mile since leaving the main road take the turning on the right (it has a waymark). You will soon cross the River Ver (there is a building on the side of bridge). Turn left here and follow the river closely upstream until you meet the main road at Bow Bridge. Cross the road and walk up the drive (once across the road you are back on a public right of way). Keep left and you will soon come to an old mill on the river, go through the gate between the mill and the farm buildings.

Note the fine chalk stream. It had been dry for many years because too much water had been extracted from the underlying chalk by water companies and farmers. Water has been put back into the headwaters and the river has new life!

3. Soon the track turns up hill to the right but continue straight on by the footpath (as shown by a waymark). When you come to a road, with a waste treatment works in an old quarry, cross the road and follow the waymark, keeping your direction.

4. Keeping the river on your left you meet a track going off to your right, carry straight on. At Redbournbury farm cross the river on a footbridge, then cross the mill stream. *On your right is an old water mill, this is being restored and is often open for inspection and has food available at certain times.* Turn into the mill grounds looking for a footpath left of the mill buildings. The river you were following is now on your left. Follow it to the main road on a clear path.

5. Cross the road and go into the farmyard opposite and look for a stile on your right. Follow this footpath for about a mile until you come to a road on the edge of Redbourn (if you turn right at this point there is a pub in about 150 yards). Cross the road and climb an embankment onto an old railway line, follow this to your left. As you walk this old railway track you are going round the edge of Redbourn. In about ³/₄ mile look out for Redbourn Church on your left, descend to it.

Redbourn is worth a visit if you have time. It has one of the finer village greens (Redbourn Common). The church has a fine oak carved screen and some interesting monuments. The main street has a variety of domestic styles and some old coaching inns.

6. Go through the churchyard with the church on your right, pass the church tower, come out of the churchyard with the motorway ahead of you and turn right keeping gardens on your right. Follow the path round, ignoring a footpath going off on your right. Finally cross a field towards the motorway following a line of telegraph posts. On reaching a road turn

left onto it and cross over the M1 motorway. Pass Flamsteadbury Farm on your left and ignore the dirt track on your left, keep to the clear farm road. In a mile there are some large concrete blocks and a road, which at this point turns a sharp corner.

7.   At this point turn sharp right off the road onto a bridleway. After about 400 yards look out for a footpath sign on your left and take this route. Drop steeply to the bottom of a valley and carry straight on ignoring a footpath to the right. When the farm track turns left go straight on, soon you will reach a road and the edge of Flamstead, turn right into the centre.

Flamstead is a pretty village with pubs and a fine church. Some wall paintings were discovered in the nave (the main body of the church). Among them is a large figure of St Christopher (15th century). Above the chancel arch and in the north east chapel there are scenes of the Last Judgement. Look at the narrow tapering spire which is known as a 'Hertfordshire Spike' a common style in the county. A village worth a visit.

Flamstead Village   © Anthony Mackay

8.   Leave the centre of the village on Holly Bush Lane, *(see map A)* heading north but turn off to the road on the left. When this road forks take the right fork and take the second footpath on the right keeping parallel to some large pylons 300 yards to your left. Keep straight on, ignoring all side paths. After crossing a small valley you are joined by a farm road from the left (³/₄ mile) keep going straight on with a hedge on your left. When you reach some allotments go round to the right, when the path divides keep to the left. On reaching the road, and Markyate, turn right to walk into the centre of this large village.

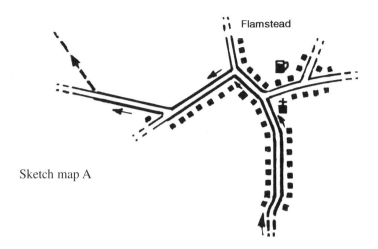

Sketch map A

Markyate is an old nucleated settlement on the main route from London to the North West. Now that it has a bypass you can enjoy its fine main street and clustered houses.

Researched and walked by Bert Richardson

Leg 6: Markyate to Tring Railway Station

Length 10 miles to Aldbury, 11 miles to Tring Station
Start Markyate **GR** 062164
Finish Aldbury **GR** 964124 Railway 951122
Maps **PFM** 1094, 1095 or E2 **LRM** 165, 166
Public Transport Markyate (see Leg 5). Aldbury local
buses only. Tring Station - National Trains
Pubs Great Gaddesden. Cafe at Monument (seasonal)
Jockey End. Also at end of walk.

The Route. This is a more wooded section of the walk and we go through
part of the Ashridge Estate with its walks, woodland and downland. Again
we cross some fine rural scenery.

*Nearby is the famous Whipsnade Zoo and Safari Park. A circular walk could be
undertaken to include the zoo or just a visit to the zoo could be arranged by the
walker.*

The Walk
1. From Markyate High Street walk down Buckwood Road to the end of
the houses. Here there is a footpath on your left with a signpost 'Roe End
Lane ³/₄ m'. Take this path up the hill, with houses on your left, and
follow it as it bears right. After about ¹/₂ mile there is a stile on your left,
cross the stile and you will come to Roe End Lane. Turn left into the lane
and pass Roe End Farm and continue to Holly Bush Lodge. Turn left on
to a wide drive signed 'To Great Gaddesden 3m' and continue, with trees
on your right and crops on your left, to Beech Wood Farm. At this point
you come to a cross roads of drives with Kennels Lodge on your left, go
left, with the lodge on your immediate right. Continue for ¹/₂ mile to
Beechwood School.

*This house was built on the site of a nunnery which, on the dissolution of the
monasteries, became a Tudor mansion where Edward VI stayed. The grounds
were designed by Capability Brown in 1754 and it became a school in 1964.*

2. Go in front of this school and turn right between the school and the
playing fields. Keeping near to the buildings (on your right) cross to the
woods (keeping an eye out for waymarks) continue through Dean Woods
to Dean Lane, a green track. Turn right on to it and in ¹/₄ mile turn left up
a few steps to a footpath that leads to Jockey End through a field and
children's playground (pub in village). Turn left on the main road and
after 100 yards on the right is a footpath signposted to Great Gaddesden.

3. This route soon opens on to green fields on a clearly marked path. You
come to a large house (The Hoo) keep straight on and you enter the edge
of a wood before descending through open fields to the road with

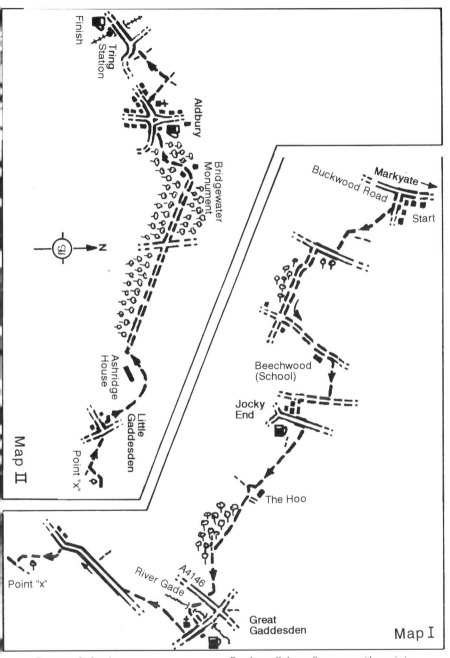

Route map for Leg 6

Based upon Ordnance Survey map with permission.
Crown copyright reserved

49

Great Gaddesden beyond. Cross the road and the River Gade, often dry, and go towards the village and the pub.

4. Go into the road named Church Meadows until you come to a path that leads across fields to St Margaret's and a road. Turn right on to this road (there is a children's farm and a Buddhist centre where visitors are welcome). Soon the tarred road peters out and you are on a farm track.

5. After ¼ mile there is a footpath bearing half left (just before some houses on your right). It crosses a very large cultivated field into a small valley where it joins another path (still in the large field). There is a small wood in the field; keep this on your left. Now climb the other side of the valley to the road on the edge of Little Gaddesden.

If you have time a detour into the village is worth while and in the church, a little detached from the village, is a memorial to the 3rd Duke of Bridgewater (see Ashridge).

6. Cross into Cromer Close opposite. Be careful here as the waymarking is not clear. On a path between houses turn right and follow this as it bears left down a hill through a wood and joins a track in the Ashridge Estate. Take the track that drops into the valley and cross by a clear path to the immediate front of Ashridge House.

We are now on the Ashridge Estate, which covers 4,000 acres of woodland and commons. It is one of the great parks of England. Its origin goes back beyond the

Ashridge House

© Nancy Scott

Middle Ages and it has developed as fashions in landscaping changed over the centuries. The estate was acquired by the National Trust in the 1920's and its many acres and miles of paths are open to the public 365 days a year (the area is rich in wildlife). Ashridge House itself started as a monastic establishment in 1276 which lasted until the dissolution in 1535. It was then owned by King Henry VIII and was a country house where the future Queen Elizabeth I stayed. Later it was the home of the Dukes of Bridgewater and the 3rd Duke was the famous Father of Inland Navigation. He built the first canal of the Industrial Age to bring coal from his mines to Manchester (1761). The house today is the result of the Gothic Revival and could be called a romantic Gothic palace with towers, turrets and a spire. It is now a management college and is not open to visitors but the immediate gardens are open to the public at certain times.

7. Walk past the front of the house and turn right to cross the edge of a golf course to come upon a magnificent straight avenue about a 1¹/₄ miles long. Follow this avenue to the Monument, a tall obelisk (see below) which can be seen in the distance.

The Monument is a Doric column surmounted by an urn, it was erected to the 3rd Duke of Bridgewater (see the piece on Ashridge). You can climb the monument at certain times on the payment of a fee. There is a National Trust cafe and an excellent information centre all open at given times (usually most weekends).

8. Follow the path in front of the information centre and you should begin to drop sharply to the village of Aldbury on a clear path. When you reach the road turn right into the village (200 yards).

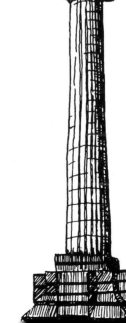

Bridgewater Monument, Ashridge Forest
© Tony Rook

Aldbury Village   © Anthony Mackay

This is a fine village with a green, complete with stocks, and village pond. There are pubs and village shops. There is a range of good domestic architecture. The church has a chapel with an excellent screen separating it from the main church. In the Verney Chapel is the tomb of Robert Whittingham killed at the Battle of Tewkesbury in 1471

9.   After passing the churchyard on your right, look for a footpath on the same side into a field with farm and house buildings on your left.   Cross by stiles but soon enter a path, to your left, with fences on both sides,   You will soon reach a T junction with a golf course beyond. Turn left and soon come to a road. Keep straight along this road to Tring Station which is the end of this leg.

Tring is 1¹/₂ miles away from the station. It is an ancient market town located in a valley where the prehistoric Icknield Way crosses the Roman Akeman Street. The Rothschild family lived at Tring Park and the second Baron founded Tring Museum, now part of the Natural History Section of the British Museum. The Tring Reservoirs are an excellent centre for birdwatching. The main railway line was built along the Bulbourne Valley in the 1830's because local landowners opposed the easier eastern route along the Gade valley. The cost of this decision was the major engineering work of Tring Cutting, some 2¹/₂ miles long, which involved the removal of 1Ω million tons of earth.

Researched and walked by Michael Blackman

Leg 7: Tring Station to Kings Langley

Length 15 miles. May be taken as two walks of about 9
miles each by taking the canal towpath at Sharpe's
Lane to Hemel Hempstead Station.
Start **Tring Station GR** 951122
Finish Kings Langley Station **GR** 080020
Maps **PFM** 1094 or **EGM** 2 and **PFM** 1119. **LRM** 165, 166
Public Transport Tring (see Leg 6). Kings Langley, train
and good local bus services.
Pubs Potten End 5 miles Bourne End 7 miles
Bovingdon 9 miles Chipperfield 12 miles

The Route. The walk goes through three pretty Chiltern villages,
extensive wooded commons (Berkhamsted Common and Chipperfield
Common), and crosses two golf courses and open farmland; there is some
road-walking which is mainly confined to quiet country lanes. Although
a long stage, this walk is easy going.

*This stage coincides in places with several other way-marked walks. A leaflet
describing the Ashridge Estate Boundary Trail may be obtained from the National
Trust Visitor Centre (01442 851227); leaflets for the Grand Union Canal Circular
Walks and the Chipperfield Common Heritage Trail, as well as more general
information, are available from Dacorum Information Centre (01442 234222).*

The Walk
1. From the entrance to Tring Station car park, turn sharp right on to a
footpath that goes diagonally across a field *(this is not a right of way but
has been used by walkers for years. If you have problems follow the road
round to the sharp left-hand bend.)* On meeting a road at a sharp bend go
south-east on a bridleway with a hedge and telegraph poles on the left.
Cross a track and leave the field by a short lane with hedges on both sides
to reach a road. Cross the road and continue on the bridleway opposite.
Go past a large house (Brightwood) and a wall on the right. At the fork,
keep to the right on an ascending path through a tunnel of trees to a
signpost. Follow the footpath to the right along the edge of the wood. The
footpath swings left through the wood and continues to climb. Emerge
from the wood on a small green, edged with white stones. Cross in front
of the gates of Toms Hill House.

2. Enter the Wood on the footpath to the left of Toms Hill House gates
*(see Sketch map A). (There are many public paths through the Ashridge
Estate, but on our route you should always be able to see open land
through the trees on your right until you reach Rail Copse).* After 150
yards on this path cross a way-marked footpath and after about another 80
yards bear right on a grass track for a further 300 yards. Turn right onto

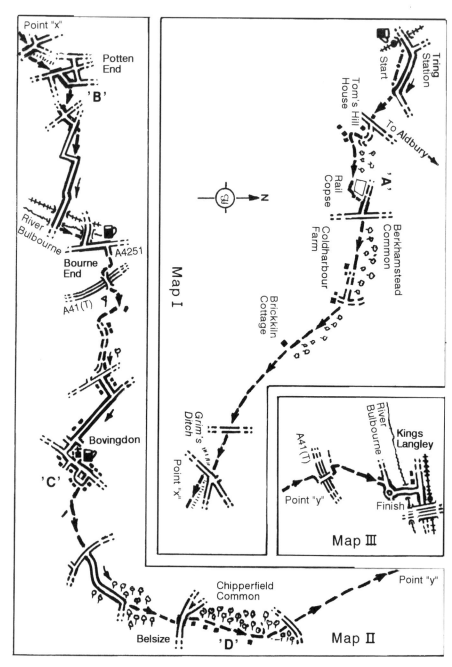

Point "x"

Potten End

'B'

River Bulbourne

A4251

Bourne End

A41(T)

Bovingdon

'C'

Tring Station

Start

Tom's Hill House

To Aldbury

Rail Copse

'A'

Coldharbour Farm

Berkhamstead Common

Brickkiln Cottage

Map I

N

Grim's Ditch

Point "x"

River Bulbourne

A41(T)

Kings Langley

Point "y"

Finish

Map III

Chipperfield Common

Point "y"

Belsize

'D'

Map II

Route map for Leg 7

Based upon Ordnance Survey map with permission.
Crown copyright reserved

54

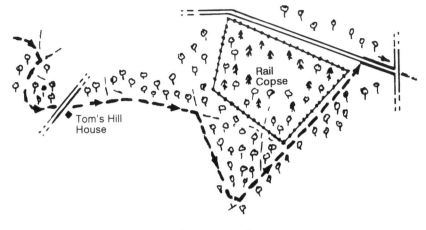

Sketch map A

the Ashridge Estate Boundary Trail (AEBT) and follow this broad track through the right hand edge of the woods for 350 yards until it forks. Take the left fork for 80 yards, then turn sharp left away from the AEBT and follow a broad ride with mature trees on the left. After 300 yards you will see the corner of Rail Copse on your left, marked by an earth bank. With the Rail Copse bank on the left, keep going in the same direction along a broad avenue between rows of mature trees.

3. Emerge at the road by a 'public bridleway' signpost. Turn right along the road to the T junction (150 yards). Cross this road (B4506) and follow the bridleway across Berkhamsted Common. At Little Coldharbour Farm join a gravel track leading towards Coldharbour Farm. Cross a track and continue in the same direction on the bridleway through the woods. Take the right fork at signpost 47. The path soon reaches the edge of the woods with open grassland on the left. Keep alongside the edge of the woods. At the end of the grassland, with Brickkiln Cottage on the right and Frithsden Beeches (National Trust woodland) on the left, follow the AEBT arrows straight ahead for about ¹/₂ mile.

Berkhamsted Common (part of the Ashridge Estate). In 1866 an attempt was made by the then-owner, Earl Brownlow, to enclose part of Berkhamsted Common. The railings he put up were removed in a single night by 120 navvies and after a long court battle the commoners, rights were upheld. The estate was later sold to pay death duties and parts of it were acquired by the National Trust in the 1920's. The area is rich in wildlife.

4. Following a bridleway sign pass between a tee and a green of a golf course on to a tree-lined path. Emerge from the trees and bear slightly to the left across the fairway to a waymark post in the trees opposite. Go through the trees, cross the road and continue on a bridleway with the golf

course on the right. Where the AEBT goes left between houses, keep straight on with the golf course still on the right. Follow the path across the fairway in front of the tee and through the woods to the road.

5. Turn right along the road for 20 yards and then left along a bridleway (Grim's Ditch) which cuts across the golf course, through woods, and then with the houses of Potten End on the left, reaches a road *(see Sketch map B)*. Turn left along the road and then first right past a green with a pond and The Red Lion pub.

Grim's Ditch extends for 16 miles from Potten End to Bradenham near High Wycombe. It is thought to be a territorial boundary from the Bronze Age.

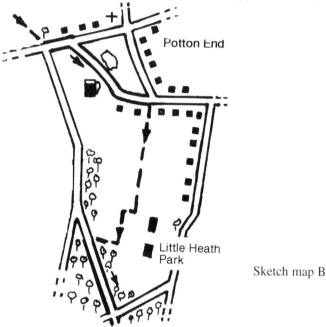

Potton End

Little Heath Park

Sketch map B

6. Continue to the end of the green and turn right along a footpath between houses. Go over a stile and continue between hedges. Go over two more stiles and follow the footpath to its end. Little Heath Park is on the left. Turn right along the gravel drive and left at the Bulbeggars sign on to a minor road. Go along the road with Little Heath on the right. Cross one road and continue straight on along the minor road to a T junction.

7. Turn right and after 50 yards turn left along a footpath through a short stretch of woodland. Go over a stile, along the edge of a field, over another stile, and diagonally across the field to a third stile. Turn right along a broad grass path for a short way and go over two stiles to reach Little Heath Lane. Turn left and continue down the lane, which affords

pleasing views across the valley, until it crosses the railway and reaches the Grand Union Canal. Cross the canal and turn right round the railings to reach the towpath. Turn right under bridge 145 and follow the towpath to bridge 146. Leave the towpath, turning right into Sharpes Lane and continue to the London road. Turn left and follow the main road past Bourne End Lane, the Anchor and the White Horse pubs.

Grand Union Canal. Originally called the Grand Junction Canal, it was part of a plan to link the Trent to the Thames. Work began in 1793. The Tring section was opened in 1799, and the whole canal, with 101 locks, was completed by 1805. The Tring Reservoirs were built to supply the canal which is 400 feet above sea level at this point. The canal was renamed the Grand Union after amalgamation with other canal companies in 1929.

8. Opposite Bourne End Hall turn right into a bridleway. Pass through a gate and follow the path to cross the A41 trunk road by a footbridge. At the far end of the bridge is a signpost pointing the route of the footpath across the golf course; the path may not be obvious, but the direction of the post accurately indicates the route which runs up the right hand side of the 14th fairway to a second signpost. Note the large house (Westbrook Hay) on your left. Go straight on, with the 14th green on the left and a spinney on the right, towards a fence and turn right on to a more obvious path. This path keeps to the left of the golf course and becomes a broad gravel track which passes two small white bungalows on the left. It then soon swings to the left round a large storage shed and joins a metalled road. Go along this road as it swings right round a putting green, and past the red brick clubhouse.

9. About 100 yards beyond the golf club car park bear left from the road onto a footpath (marked by a signpost) which cuts through the edge of Gorsefield Wood. Where the footpath emerges from the trees, turn right into Hempstead Road then immediately left into Bushfield Road. At the far end of Bushfield Road turn right into Stoney Lane and continue along this lane into Bovingdon *(see Sketch map C)*. Enter the churchyard by the lych gate and follow the path past the church to Church Street. Turn left past the Bull pub into Chipperfield Road and after about 250 yards turn right into a small housing estate, Austins Mead, at the signpost to Bovingdon Green.

Bovingdon. The present church, rebuilt in 1845 on the site of a 13th century church, contains the medieval tomb of a 14th century knight. It has one of the largest churchyards in the county. In the centre of the village is a pentagonal wooden wellhouse, erected in 1881 in memory of Sir Granville Rider of Westbrook Hay.

10. At the far side of Austins Mead take the footpath between two houses, cross a stile and keep to the path along the right hand edge of the field. Go over another stile and bear left diagonally across the field. Cross the

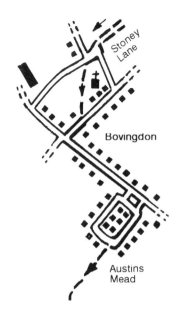

Sketch map C

Stoney Lane

Bovingdon

Austins Mead

stile, keep to the left of the field along a barbed wire fence then right along the far side of the same field to a stile by some trees. Cross into the next field and keep to the left hand edge of this field with a hedge at your left. At the end of the hedge go in the same direction across the middle of an open field. The path continues along the right hand side of the field with a fence and trees on the right. Leave the field by a stile, cross the road and continue along Holly Hedges Lane.

Wooden Well House, Bovingdon,
built in 1881

© Nancy Scott

58

11. After passing Hollow Hedge cottage on the left, the lane enters Woodman's Wood. Leave the lane where it turns sharply right, and go straight ahead along a broad path, signposted 'Belsize ³/₄'. Where the path forks, keep to the left and then to the left hand edge of the field as the path emerges from the trees. Turn left into Dunny Lane and after 50 yards or so, at the foot of Windmill Hill, turn right up a narrow bridleway which climbs through the trees of Chipperfield Common *(see Sketch map D).*

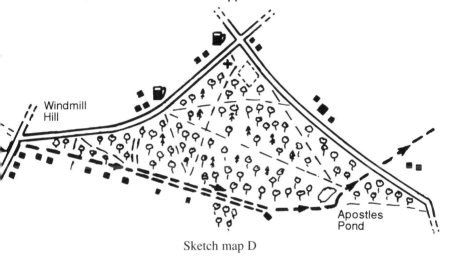

Sketch map D

Chipperfield The village, with its church (1837), cricket field and pubs lies at the northern apex of the common. The wooded common (116 acres) was under royal ownership from the 13th to the 16th century. It contains two prehistoric burial mounds. On the southern edge is the Apostles Pond, so called because of the 12 surrounding lime trees planted 1714. In the 1980's the original trees were pollarded, and twelve new trees were planted.

12. There are many paths through the trees across the common; the most direct route follows the bridleway at the right hand edge of the common with houses to the right until it reaches the Apostles Pond. A few paces beyond the pond, with a 6-barred iron gate on your right, bear half left away from the bridleway along a narrow path through the trees. This path is not very distinct, but goes in a NE direction, soon crossing another path at a signpost marked '6 Turn Around'. Do not turn around, but keep going in a NE direction, to cross a broad bridleway and emerge from the common at Top Common.

13. Cross the road and enter a footpath at a stile to the left of the entrance drive for The Paddock; this footpath is signposted 'Kings Langley 1³/₄'. In quick succession the footpath crosses four more stiles, and then follows the left hand edge of a field, crossing yet another stile and then

descending the left hand edge of another field. At the bottom of the descent the path runs through an archway of overhanging branches, crosses a stile and ascends a gentle slope along the right hand edge of a field. Leave this field by a gate and continue along a broad farm track. After 100 yards or so, leave this track, climb over a stile on the left (just by a 7-barred iron gate) and continue along the footpath which runs parallel to the farm track. After three more stiles, the path enters a field; the path here is not very distinct, but keep going in the same direction towards a stile which is clearly visible in the opposite hedge. Cross this stile and another field, aiming towards a stile in the far fence, using a distant radio mast as a marker.

14. Turn right to cross the A41 by a footbridge. At the far side of the footbridge turn left and after 50 yards cross a stile into a field. Keep to the left hand edge of this field and descend along a broad track which eventually reaches Kings Langley at the Watford Road, between Broadfield Farm and Wayside Farm. Turn right along the main road for 100 yards, then left down a footpath just before the roundabout. At the bottom of the footpath join the main road across the canal and continue to the T-junction with Station Road. The entrance to the station car park is directly opposite and Kings Langley station is about 150 yards to the right along Station Road.

Kings Langley. Langley was held by Robert de Mortain, a half brother of William the Conqueror in 1086 (Domesday Book). Queen Eleanor of Castile, wife of Edward I, bought the manor for £20 in 1276, and converted it to a royal palace. For the next two centuries it was a major royal residence. Edward II spent much time there with his notorious friend, Piers Gaveston. Gaveston was buried at Langley Priory after being beheaded. Edmund de Langley (son of Edward III), the first Duke of York, was born at the palace in 1341, died there in 1401, and is buried in the parish church. Richard II was also born at the palace, and was buried at the priory after being murdered, but his remains were later reburied in Westminster Abbey. Henry V bestowed Langley Palace on Queen Joan of Navarre; Henry VIII gave it to three of his wives in succession, but none of them ever lived there. What little remains of the priory, and the site of the royal palace, are to be found at the top of Langley Hill (grid ref.: 065026). Paper making came to the area in the 18th century when John Dickinson converted two medieval corn mills on the River Gade. The Ovaltine factory and model dairy farm were built in 1913.

Researched and walked by Sue and Peter Garside

Leg 8: Kings Langley to Shenley

Length 12½ miles
Start Kings Langley Railway Station **GR** 080020
Finish Shenley, Black Lion PH **GR** 188008
Maps **PFM** 1119 & 1139 **LRM** 166
Public Transport (See Leg 7) for Kings Langley. Shenley:
    local bus services. Radlett Station 2¼ miles
Pubs Round Bush 7½ miles, Letchmore Heath 8 miles

The Route. The most powerful influence on the landscape of southern Hertfordshire is London. Since Roman times, London has been the stimulus for building traffic routes northwards through the county and for the concentration of centres of population within easy travelling distance of the capital. The walk from Kings Langley to Shenley threads its way, mostly along green belt, between the southern edges of Hemel Hempstead and St Albans (to the north) and Abbots Langley and the northern suburbs of Watford (to the south). Although the M25 shares this corridor, and the walk also crosses the M1, the A405 London orbital road and the three main railway lines from London to the north, the traffic and the towns are mostly out-of-sight, if not always out of ear-shot. Much of the way is through open farmland, parkland and woods.

The Walk

1. Turn right into Station Road outside Kings Langley Station. *Using permissive paths through Numbers Farm:* about 250 yards beyond the entrance to the Station car park turn right onto a minor road opposite Roman Gardens. Go under the railway arch and immediately turn left onto a grassy farm track. Follow this track between fields towards Numbers Farm. Turn right in front of a wooden barn, following the main track which becomes a public footpath east of the farm.

Alternative route if the permissive path is no longer viable. Continue along Station Road for about 550 yards beyond Roman Gardens, passing the Ovaltine Factory on your left, then turn right onto Tom's Lane under the narrow railway arch. There is no pavement under the arch so beware of traffic. Immediately after house number 38 on the right hand side, turn onto a bridleway and follow this across the fields until it joins the farm track east of Numbers Farm.

2. Continue along this track. keeping roughly parallel to the M25 (on the right) for about a mile. About 100 yards before reaching a large shed on the right, turn left onto a marked footpath. Follow this path across a field through the hedge and across a stile. Cross the next field diagonally to the far right corner and, passing between a children's play area on the right and a sportsfield on the left, turn into a residential road, Meadow Way, at

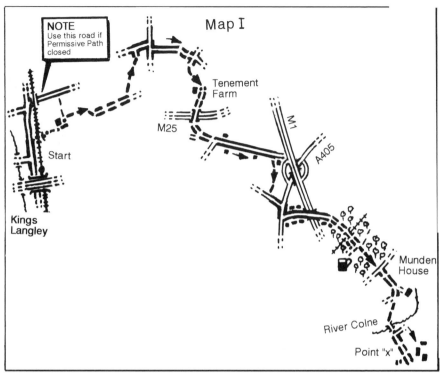

Map I

NOTE
Use this road if
Permissive Path
closed

Tenement
Farm

M25

M1

A405

Start

Kings
Langley

Munden
House

River Colne

Point "x"

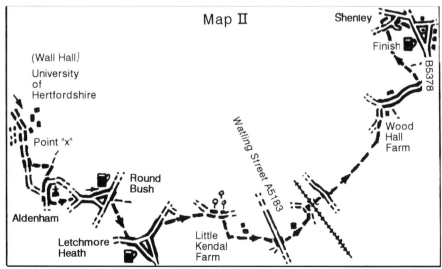

Map II

Shenley

Finish

B5378

(Wall Hall)
University
of
Hertfordshire

Point "x"

Watling Street A5183

Wood
Hall
Farm

Round
Bush

Aldenham

Letchmore
Heath

Little
Kendal
Farm

Route map for Leg 8

The former Ovaltine Model Dairy near Kings Langley   © Anthony Mackay

the entrance to Bedmond JMI school. Go along Meadow Way and turn right at the T-junction along Tom's Lane into Bedmond.

Bedmond/Abbots Langley. Abbots Langley was so named because it was owned by the Abbot of St. Albans. In the parish church is a memorial tablet to Nicholas Breakspear, the only English pope. He became pope in 1154, and took the name of Adrian IV. Breakspear was not born in Abbots Langley itself, but in the neighbouring hamlet of Bedmond. An Abbots Langley mother, Elizabeth Greenhill (d. 1681), holds the British record for the greatest number of confinements. She had 39 children in 38 confinements, which meant she was pregnant every year from 16 to 54. Equally amazing for that period, all her offspring survived to adulthood.

3. At the roundabout turn right along the main road and then left along a bridleway just before the Bell pub. After about ¼ mile, at the entrance to Ninnings Farm, go through a kissing gate and take the footpath diagonally left into the trees, passing through a latched wooden gate. Go through another kissing gate, then keep to the right-hand path through the trees and turn right where this meets another path at right angles. After crossing a stile adjacent to a gate, exit from the trees onto an open field. Aim to cross the field between two large oak trees towards a gate. Cross the stile to the right of the gate, go over the lane in front of Tenements Farm, and cross another stile into a field. Cross the field to the right of a large oak tree to another gate with a stile on its right. Leave the field by the stile and turn left along a bridleway, which swings round and crosses the M25 by a bridge. *Weather permitting, the squat water tower of Shenley hospital may be seen on the skyline almost due east of this bridge;*

63

4. Keep along the bridleway, ignoring footpaths to the right, until it joins Chequers Lane at a gate. Continue in the same direction along the lane. Take care, as this is a narrow lane which has quite a steady flow of traffic at times. Pass Waterdale House on the right. Immediately past a whitewashed cottage (The Chequers) take the narrow footpath signposted to the right. Cross a stile, turn right to enter a field and then go up the left hand edge of this field. Turn left to leave the field by a stile at the top left hand corner and keep left along a path with overhanging hedges on both

The white washed cottage, (Chequers)   © Nancy Scott

sides. Cross a stile into a large field and go diagonally due south across the field passing to the left of the leftmost tree, to an improvised stile in a barbed wire fence. Go over this and bear slightly right to cross the school playing field towards high green railings. Go through a gap to the left of the railings and along a broad grass strip towards more railings (a crematorium is on the left).

5. Beyond these railings turn left into High Elms Lane. At the T-junction turn right along the A405 and cross it by a subway. Go up the slope to Bucknalls Lane and turn left along it following the signpost to the Building Research Establishment. Continue along this road across the M1 and keep straight on until the road narrows. Take the bridleway to the right along the edge of Bricket Wood Common. Follow the bridleway through the common.

Bricket Wood. A large wooded common where the River Ver meets the Colne.

6. Cross the railway line by a red brick bridge. A muddy section of the bridleway has wooden sleepers to make the way easier. Cross a signposted footpath and continue to School Lane. Cross this and continue opposite by a notice to Munden. Go along the gravel track. Turn right over a stile, at a signpost to Aldenham, into parkland. Cross this diagonally (south) crossing Munden House drive by a signpost and continuing to an iron footbridge over the River Colne.

Munden House. An early 19th century Gothic mansion.

7. Follow the well-trodden path to another footbridge over a dry gulch. Continue in the same direction with a golf course on the right. Leave the track to the left of an iron gate. Continue in the same direction on a road through the University of Hertfordshire, Wall Hall College grounds.

Wall Hall. The house was built in 1802 when the Gothic revival style was in fashion. It was then called Aldenham Abbey. A sham ruin was also built, parts of which came from Aldenham Church. Wall Hall became a teacher training college in 1945 and is now part of the University of Hertfordshire.

8. At a junction take the road to the right in front of a black wooden barn and continue on the road past a fitness centre. At a mini-roundabout go straight along the road towards Aldenham Church. Turn left on a footpath across a field towards a pylon. Turn right before a stile and continue along the left hand edge of the field.

Aldenham Church. The church of St John is 13th century with numerous later additions. It is partly faced with Hertfordshire pudding stone, a conglomerate

Aldenham Church   © Anthony Mackay

Aldenham War Memorial Hall, Letchmore Heath © Nancy Scott

stone unique to Hertfordshire. It has a needle spire rising from the centre of the tower roof, well within the parapet; such spires are a peculiarity of the county, and are known as Hertfordshire spikes.

9. At the end of the field carry on between houses towards the church. Cross the road and enter the churchyard. Follow the path round the church and on through the churchyard. Where the path turns to the right, keep going straight ahead along a grassy path with a red brick wall on the left. Cross Church Lane and continue along the main road to Round Bush. Immediately after passing the signpost to Letchmore Heath and Aldenham School, veer to the right away from the main road, keeping the row of houses on your right. Cross Summerhouse Lane and enter the field at the right-hand of two gateways. Follow the bridleway signposted 'Letchmore Heath ½ mile'. At the end of the bridleway turn left into Grange Lane.

Letchmore Heath. This is a picturesque village with a green, a village pond, and timber-framed cottages dating from the 16th and 17th centuries. As well as the war memorial on the green, the village honoured its dead of the 1914-18 war by placing plaques on the houses of those who lost their lives. Each has the words 'Lest We Forget' and gives the name of the soldier who left that house for the war, never to return. The International Society for Krishna Consciousness occupies Bhaktivedanta Manor (formerly Piggott's Manor) on the southern edge of the village.

10. Take the right fork into the village to see the pond and the green. Cross the green by the war memorial and turn left into Back Lane, then turn right into Common Lane. Just before reaching the overhead power cables, leave the lane along a gravel track to the right, go through a gate marked 'The Cottage' and then over a low railing to the left of double white iron gates. Follow the gravel track to its end between a house on the left and a whitewashed building on the right. Go through a double wooden gate, then a small latched wooden gate, and cross a strip of grass, through another double wooden gate and along a short gravel track. Go through a wooden gate at the side of a five barred gate, cross a small metalled lane, and continue in the same direction along the gravel track with a field on the right and stables on the left.

11. The path narrows past a small bungalow on the left, and continues with barbed wire on the right and wire netting on the left. Cross a stile, turn sharp left and then sharp right onto a path between rows of trees. Cross a stile and go along the left hand edge of a large field. Cross another stile and carry on in the same direction. Turn left across a stile onto a broad track which joins from the left and continue right along this track. Where the track passes a small wood on the left hand side, turn right onto the footpath which crosses a large field.

12. At the far side of the field turn left beside a large oak tree. Ignore the first stile on the right (35 yards beyond the oak tree) and keep to the field edge for another 85 yards. Cross the stile in the hedge just past another large oak tree; this takes you into the corner of a grassy field. Head just south of east towards the centre of the hedge in the opposite side, where there is a stile. Cross the stile and continue through the middle of the long narrow field with the brick buildings of Little Kendals Farm on the left. As the field widens, keep to the middle of the fleld aiming slightly to the left of the large dead tree and continue in the same direction to the patchy hedge at the bottom of the slope. Cross a small concrete bridge and head across the field to the stile in the hedge opposite.

13. Cross this stile into Watling Street. Cross Watling Street, turn right for 100 yards and then turn left along a metalled road signposted to Stanley House Country Club and Kendal Hall. Where the road turns left to the Country Club, keep straight on for 50 yards to reach a stile at the right hand side of the farm lane. Cross the stile. Keeping the line of the pylons and power cables to your right, cross towards the bottom left hand corner of the field. Cross the stile and enter a strip of scrub. Turn left onto a narrow footpath through the scrub with fields on the left. Emerge at a rutted farm track by a seven barred gate and a stile. Turn left along the track with the railway line on your right. Where the track turns left away from the railway, turn right over a stile and go under the railway arch. Continue on a grass track, crossing a footbridge. Turn right

through the hedge, then left along the field with a hedge on the left until reaching a road.

Watling Street was the longest of the Roman roads in Britain, running from Dover, through London to Chester. Much of the original Roman road (including this section through southern Hertfordshire) is still part of major highways.

14. Cross the road with care as this is a blind corner with fast-moving traffic. Cross a stile beside a fence marked private. Soon cross another stile by a derelict shed. Cross the field aiming for a wide gap in the hedge, cross a footbridge over a ditch, and cross the next field near the left hand side. Go left over a footbridge and leave the field by a stile onto a path between hedges. Follow this path until it meets a track. Cross the stile, turn right and follow the track between farm buildings. Turn right into a lane and continue for about 1/2 mile. Turn left through a kissing gate into a strip of woodland following a footpath signposted to Radlett Lane.

15. Continue in this direction, ignoring a right turning, though the strip of woodland to a stile. Cross this into a field and keep along the right hand edge. At the corner of the field, go through a large gap in the hedge by two dead trees and continue in the same direction across the middle of the next field to reach a stile. Cross Radlett Lane and enter Shenley Park by another stile. Turn left and in a few yards cross over a wooden footbridge and immediately turn right along a narrow gravel path. Follow this footpath until it rejoins Radlett Lane. Cross over the Lane, go through a staggered wooden gate and follow the path to reach the road opposite the Black Lion.

Shenley. Near the War Memorial stands an 18th century lock-up. Porters Park, dating from the 13th century, was a large estate on the north-west edge of Shenley. This was the home of the architect, Nicholas Hawksmoor (d. 1736), who was Wren's assistant on St. Paul's. Admiral Lord Howe also lived there. He was First Lord of the Admiralty when Nelson was in his twenties and was made Admiral of the Fleet in 1796. A mental hospital, opened by King George V and Queen Mary in 1934, occupied part of the estate until 1996. The hospital water tower remains as a prominent landmark. Shenley Park has been created as part of the redevelopment of Shenley Hospital; excellent leaflets are available from the park office just off Radlett Lane.

Further Information. Information about the Shenley Park Trust may be obtained from the Director on 01923 852629.

Researched and walked by Sue and Peter Garside

The 18th century lock-up, Shenley © Nancy Scott

Leg 9: Shenley to Cuffley

Length   10 miles
Start   The Black Lion Pub Shenley **GR** 188008
Finish   Cuffley Station **GR** 307028
Maps   **PFM** 1119 & 1120 **LRM** 166
Public Transport   Shenley (see Leg 8) Cuffley - mainline
     trains and local buses.
Pubs   Shenley, Blackhorse Lane 3 miles, Northaw 7miles
     and Cuffley.

The Route.   On this walk we cross trunk road and railway routes radiating from London - M25, A1(M), the old Great North Road at Potters Bar and two railway routes from Kings Cross/Moorgate. But it is surprising how rural this walk is and the variety of scenery to be experienced.

The Walk
1. At the Black Lion Pub start down the hill on the right hand side (Black Lion Hill) along the B5378 for about half a mile in the direction of St Albans, until you come to a bus shelter. Where the path stops carry on a rough track along the roadside

2. On the right hand side of the road climb up the bank to join the footpath at the post and sign. Soon after you join the path you come to a waymark post where you bear right to follow the crossfield path. There are two sets of overhead lines in front of you. Make for the left hand wooden post of the nearer overhead lines. You will see a waymark post. At this point you go through a small, overgrown piece of copse and in the next field is another crossfield path. Make for the right hand edge of the woodland you see in front of you.

3. At the waymark post at the farm track turn right for 15 yards or so on this path, until you see a stile on your left. This leads to another crossfield path. Bear slightly right and make for the middle of the woodland you see in front of you. At the next stile bear half right towards the right hand edge of the copse, walk past the abandoned brick building and, keeping to the same line, cross the farm track and make for and cross the stile. Keeping the post and rail fence on your right, walk through the stand of trees and cross the stile at the bend in the farm track. Follow the track up to a stile on your left, opposite the barn (Shenley Stud Farm). Cross the stile and a small field takes you on to Rectory Lane.

4. Ignore the stile and signpost in front of you. Turn left along Rectory Lane, past the 'Gallops for hire' notice on your right for 250 yards as far as 'Grassfields' on your left. Cross the stile opposite (post and sign) and make for and cross the stile at the bottom left hand corner of the field.

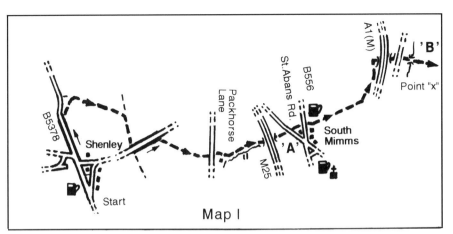

Map I

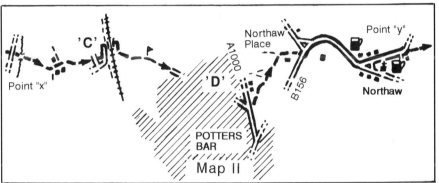

Map II

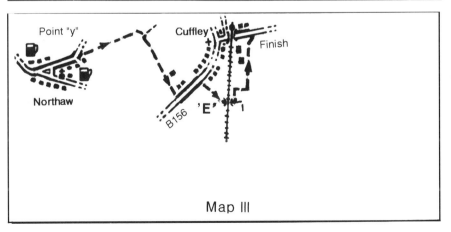

Map III

Route map for Leg 9

Based upon Ordnance Survey map with permission.
Crown copyright reserved

Follow a fence on your left to an unlocked metal gate and stile at a narrow tarred lane (Dovers Green). Cross two stiles opposite. Walk straight across an open field following the overhead lines to a stile at the far left corner. Follow the hedge on your left in the next field and two stiles bring you to Packhorse Lane alongside Rabley Park Farm.

5. Cross the road and stile opposite, near the post and sign 'Public Footpath to S. Mimms ¾ mile'. Cross an open field bearing right to a gate and stile. Cross over to take the stile on your immediate left into a field, turn right and follow a fence down to the stream (Catherine Bourne) and follow the stream with it on your right. The next stretch to the M25 should not present any difficulties *(see Sketch map A)*. You simply walk alongside the Bourne on your right. After the M25 subway you continue, keeping the Bourne on your right, until you get to the next road (St. Albans Road).

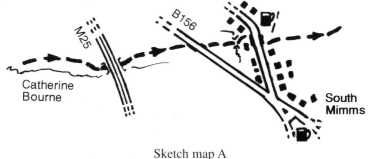

Sketch map A

6. Cross over to the signpost (almost opposite) and follow the Bourne again but keeping it now on your left for the next short stretch. Cross the small concrete bridge (no handrails) and then walk between two gardens and houses to join Blackhorse Lane.

The Black Horse pub is across the road on your left. The road to your right leads to South Mimms Village, Ridge, M25 services and the B556 to Potters Bar. Blackhorse Lane on your left leads, eventually, to the M25 at London Colney.

7. Cross the road, walk 25 yards to your right and on your left you will see a tarred lane between houses with a signpost at the end at a stile. One arm *'No. 30 Rabley Park'* points back the way you have come, a second points half left to 'North Mimms', and there should be a third arm (currently missing) pointing straight on to Warrengate Farm, this is the way you should go. Follow the hedge on your right for 200 yards, then ahead of you is a large metal pylon; cross to it and you are on a wide track. Make for the A1(M) on this track. The Bourne is about 100 yards on your right along this stretch. When you get to the A1(M) boundary you follow it until you get to the road subway. Go through the subway and almost immediately after the subway you cross the old A1 and enter the field opposite by a stile *(see Sketch map B)*.

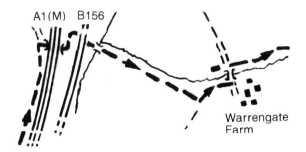

A1(M) B156

Sketch map B

Warrengate
Farm

8. Use the footbridge in front of you to cross the ford of Mimmshall Brook. Go straight ahead with the stream on your left until you reach Warrengate Farm. Cross the brook there and turn immediately right *(see Sketch map C)*. Keep this brook on your right until you reach the Cranbourne Industrial Estate road. Cross the road to the signpost opposite and a short stretch of path to bring you to another road. Turn left and walk for approximately 50 yards to a subway under the railway. This brings you to the Potters Bar Golf Course.

Potters
Bar

Sketch map C

Cranbourne
Ind. Estate

9. Turn right on to the golf course keeping the railway embankment on your immediate right at the stile. When you come to a large diameter pipe go under it and you should now see a series of waymarks with a ditch on your right. You pass a number of footbridges (12 of them!). Watch out for the waymark that points right over a grassed bridge (the 12th, a brick built drainage channel). Cross at this point and you enter a path leading up the slope through the trees. You come out into a very short drive with gates to your left, turn right here and then left on to Mountway.

10. You will come to the junction of Darkes Lane and Church Road *(If you wish to go to Potters Bar for the railway and bus stations, shops etc turn right here into Darkes Lane and continue for ¹/₂ mile but return here to continue the route).* Go into Church Road opposite and look out for Quakers Lane on your right. Follow Quakers Lane to its junction with Hatfield Road and look for a kissing gate opposite *(see Sketch map D)*. Join the path at a kissing gate.

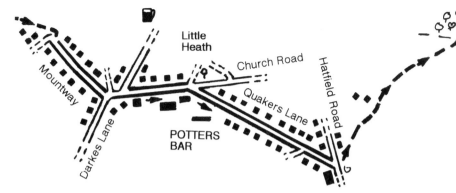

Little
Heath

Church Road

Hatfield Road

Quakers Lane

Mountway

POTTERS
BAR

Darkes Lane

Sketch map D

Potters Bar. First recorded in 1387, refers to a former gate between estates along the Great North Road. It owes its development from a small hamlet initially to the Great North Road and later, from 1852, to the railway from London which turned it into a commuter town. It has a population of 22,000.

11. Follow a well defined path ahead of you and, ignoring a stile on your left, go through the opening in the hedge and turn sharp right following the hedge on your right. After 50 yards or so, ignore the opening in front of you and turn left, keeping the hedge and barbed wire fence on your right, again following a well defined path. Cross the stile and follow the path at the right edge of a small stretch of woodland until you get to an open field. Northaw House and some new properties will be diagonally right of you. Follow a well defined path and, at the bottom left of the field, cross a footbridge then bear right. With the gardens immediately on your right you come out on to Coopers Lane at St. Just.

12. At the junction of Well Road, Coopers Lane and Judges Hill cross over and turn left along Judges Hill. Walk straight ahead along Judges Hill to Northaw Village Green, War Memorial, church and two pubs. Go left at the Sun pub, down Vineyards Road for about 650 yards to a stile on the right next to Carramore House, pointing to Cuffley (see Sketch map E). Follow the path down to the valley across stiles gradually dropping to the valley bottom. Cross a footbridge and turn right following the Cuffley Brook on your right. At a junction of the paths carry straight on along the farm track for æ mile to Northaw Road East.

Northaw is a Conservation area. It has a long history linked with the Abbot and monks of St. Albans Abbey certainly from about 800 AD to 1539 when the Abbey lands were dissolved. The church is Victorian, the old one was burnt down in 1881. The attraction of Northaw Common was initially as a hunting area with Enfield Chase also on its borders. Northaw became popular with the gentry and a number of fine houses survive. On this route you pass Northaw Place, now a residential development, and Northaw House, the base for ACP (Architects Partnership).

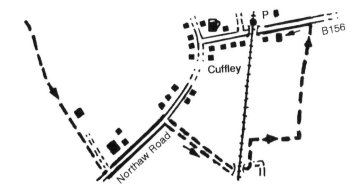

Sketch map E

The Kings Well was a chalybeate spring (iron salts rich), popular with James 1 and Charles II and the gentry. Charles had a large marquee erected there for their accommodation. It was still famous enough in 1809 to get a special mention in John Cary's Map of Hertfordshire. The name still survives in Cuffley street names like Kingswell Drive. Along this stretch you pass the Pumping Station on your left. The site of The King's Well is not precisely known but was in the area of the Pumping Station.

13. Go left along the road for about 150 yards passing playing fields on your right to a signpost at the main entrance to the playing fields and car park. Turn right and follow the track under the railway bridge (at the toilet sign before the main entrance you can turn into the playing fields to cross to the footpath and save a little road walking).

14. Turn immediately left at the waymarks. Follow the hedge parallel to the railway then at right angles along the field edge to a stile. Cross the

Northaw Village   © Nancy Scott

stile and follow the line of the hedge on your left until you come to commercial buildings and a petrol station on your left and the Youth Centre on your right. Join Cuffley Hill left, to the village and railway station car park. The Cuffley, now a Harvesters, is on your right 50 yards beyond the railway bridge.

Cuffley. Evidence of prehistoric and some Roman activity has been discovered in the area. It gained national fame in September 1916 when the first German Zeppelin destroyed in this country was shot down near the Plough pub in Cuffley by the night fighter pilot William Leefe Robinson VC whose memorial is on East Ridgeway. It is near the pub and his name survives as a Cuffley street name. Cuffley, with the arrival of the railway in 1909, began to develop as a commuter village and particularly in the last sixty years has rapidly expanded with quite a range of shops in the village centre.

Northaw Great Wood lies between Cuffley and Northaw and, with its three marked circular paths, is very popular with local people as a leisure resource for walking and relaxation.

Researched and walked by Hywel Morris

Leg 10: Cuffley to Hertford

Length 13 miles
Start   Cuffley Railway Station **GR** 307028
Finish   Parliament Square, Hertford **GR** 326125
Maps   **PFM** 1096 & 1120   **LRM** 166
Public Transport   Cuffley (see Leg 9) Hertford - two main
line stations with different routes and a bus station
Pubs   several on route from Newgate Street at 2 miles.

The Route. Starting from Cuffley, the route goes somewhat west of north through Newgate Street to West End. From there it proceeds in an easterly direction through Essendon and Little Berkhamsted to Bayford. It finally goes in a northerly direction to Hertford. The route takes us through several pretty villages.

The Walk

1. On leaving Cuffley Station, turn right and in 80 yards turn right again along Tolmers Road. Follow this to its end (about 1mile) and continue along a footpath running uphill into a wood with a fence on the right. On reaching a road, turn right and follow the road uphill for about half a mile to Newgate Street. Turn left at the roundabout and in 50 yards take the left fork, New Park Road.

2. Follow this to the end of the houses and continue straight on along a track. In about half a mile follow the track round a corner to the right and then continue straight on and emerge between houses on to a road. Turn left along the road and in 30 yards take the right fork (Cucumber Lane). After half a mile take the bridleway on the left and follow it along the inside edge of the wood. Continue uphill through trees and bushes, passing several houses on the left, to reach a road.

3. Go straight across onto a public footpath and then turn right in 150 yards at buildings. Keep going downhill to emerge in a field and continue down with the hedge on the left to a gap in the bottom hedge. Through the gap, turn left on to a footpath into a wood (do not cross the bridge). Proceed along the path, crossing a wooden bridge, and keep straight on to emerge into a field. Go up the left hand edge of the field. About 15 yards from the corner of the field, on a downward slope, turn left through a gap in the hedge on to a track and go right along the track for about half a mile. Turn left at a waymark (yellow arrow) and follow the footpath through a few trees and then along the edge of a field with the hedge on the right. Cross two stiles and reach a road at West End by the Candlestick pub.

4. Turn right along the road and in a quarter of a mile take the byway to the right. After half a mile, take the path to the left. Proceed downhill with the hedge on the left, cross a bridge, bear diagonally left, and take

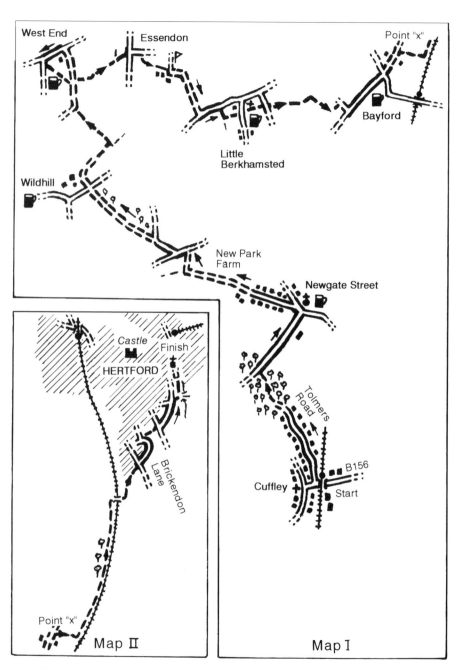

West End
Essendon
Point "x"
Bayford
Little
Berkhamsted
Wildhill
New Park
Farm
Newgate Street
Tolmers
Road
Castle
Finish
HERTFORD
Brickendon
Lane
B156
Cuffley
Start
Point "x"
Map II
Map I

Route map for Leg 10

Based upon Ordnance Survey map with permission.
Crown copyright reserved

West End, The Candlestick © Nancy Scott

the footpath uphill through the wood. Emerge by the pavilion of Essendon Cricket Club and follow the edge of a field, with a wall on the right, to a road. Turn left, then in 50 yards turn right along School Lane. Pass the village hall on the left and in 40 yards take the footpath to the right (signposted Little Berkhamsted 1 mile). Follow the path into the golf course (ignore a right fork), pass in front of the clubhouse, and follow the waymarked path to reach white buildings at the bottom of the hill.

Essendon has the Salisbury Crest inn (now a private dwelling) which dates from the 17th century, and a church which has several monumental brasses. Look for a stone on the outside commemorating repairs after a Zeppelin raid in the First World War.

5. Go between the buildings and take the path going diagonally right uphill behind the cottage and follow it past farm buildings to emerge on a road. Turn left and in 100 yards turn right onto a bridleway. In 50 yards cross a stile on the left into Little Berkhamsted Cricket Club ground and follow the left hand edge of the ground to the road. Turn left along the road and in 50 yards turn right (just before the churchyard) and pass through a kissing gate onto a public footpath. Follow this through a further gate and over a stile to a road.

Little Berkhamsted has the Five Horseshoes which is even older than the former inn at Essendon. Look out, while in this area, for the noted landmark Stratton's

Little Berkhamsted

© Nancy Scott

Observatory built in 1789, a folly in the form of a five-storey tower built by retired admiral John Stratton, which can be seen from miles around.

6. Turn right and in 15 yards turn left to cross a stile on to a footpath (signposted Bayford 1 mile). After two further stiles, the path bears diagonally left across fields passing the corner of a wood. Continue over a bridge into a wood. In about 200 yards the path turns right and then left at waymarks. Continue uphill across a track and shortly cross a stile into a field. Follow the field edge with the hedge on the left and cross a stile at the field corner onto a path which quickly becomes a track and follow this to a road (Ashendene Road).

7. Turn left along the road and proceed into Bayford. Pass the Bakers Arms on the right and continue straight on along Bayford Green. The road bends right and then left between buildings and continues as a track between trees. In 100 yards take the footpath on the right crossing a stile (signposted Hertford). At the end of the field cross a stile on the right and go down the next field with a wire fence on the left. Enter a small wood and cross a stile on the left into a long field.

The church of St Mary at Bayford dates only from 1870 but it is built on the site of two early churches and contains relics from them including a 15th century font. There are some very pretty cottages around the pond.

8. Follow the edge of this field with a wire fence (and a railway line) on the right for about æ mile. About 100 yards from the end of the field, the path crosses a wooden footbridge on the right and continues in the same direction through woods with the railway on the right for a further mile. After a short section between wire-mesh fences on both sides, turn right and cross the railway track by a footbridge. Follow the path to the left across two fields to a road.

9. Turn left at the road and then right up Mandeville Road. Follow this for about ¹/₂ mile, turn right into Wilton Crescent, and in 20 yards right again into a footpath. Pass a school on the left and at the end of the path cross the road into Queens Road. Just past the junction with Highfield Road (entering from the left), turn right through barriers and follow the path down. At the bottom of the hill turn left and continue with the stream on the right. Reach and continue along a road and at the 'T' junction cross straight over and take the footpath through the churchyard. Swing left round the church, and leave by the main gate. Take the underpass on the right, walk down Church Street to the Shire Hall (not County Hall the modern administrative centre for the county) and turn left to go into Parliament Square.

Information on Hertford is given in the introduction to Leg 11.

10. To go to Hertford East railway station and the bus station, go along the right hand side of the Shire Hall, cross the Square to the far right corner and proceed along Railway Street. The bus station is along the first road to the left. For the railway station, continue along the road and go left at the roundabout. The station is a further 200 yards on the left. For Hertford North station, go to the right out of Parliament Square and follow this road (The Wash, then St Andrew's Street, then North Road) for about ³/₄ mile.

Researched and walked by Nancy and Michael Scott

Leg 11: Hertford to Widford

Length 13½ miles
Start Hertford Parliament Square **GR** 326125
Finish Widford (village centre) **GR** 420159
Maps **PFM** 1096 & 1097 **LRM** 166
Public Transport Hertford - see Leg 10 Widford limited
      local buses
Pubs **GR** 322168 ¾ mile after Stapleford, Wadesmill,
      Wareside.

The Route. From Hertford the walk goes in a northerly direction through Waterford to Stapleford and then proceeds easterly through Tonwell, Wadesmill, Thundridge and Wareside to Widford. This is an entirely rural walk once we leave the environment of Hertford.

Hertford has a long history, claiming, though not without dispute, to be the site of the first National Synod in AD 673, and there is evidence for a small Roman settlement before this. In AD 912/3 two burghs or fortified settlements were established on the north and south banks of the River Lea. That on the south bank was replaced by a Norman motte and bailey and this by a major castle late in the 12th century. Of this, much of the flint curtain wall survives. What is now called Hertford castle is a gatehouse erected in the 15th century. Hertford has many other old buildings and, as an old coaching town, many inns and public houses. It has a small but active museum.

The Walk

1. Leave Parliament Square by The Wash, turn right at the traffic lights and follow the road (Old Cross, then Cowbridge, then Portvale, then Molewood Road) straight along for about ¾ mile. Continue in the same direction when the road becomes a lane and then a track to meet the main road. Turn right and follow the road. Pass Great Molewood branching off to the right and in 50 yards take the footpath on the right through trees onto Waterford Marsh.

Waterford Marsh includes grazing land free to all parishioners and the church has a remarkable collection of stained glass by famous artists.

2. Continue along the path with the river on the left to Waterford. At the road turn right and in 50 yards turn left into Barleycroft. At its end cross a 'lifting' stile and go straight ahead across the field to a second stile and over it to follow a path through a wood to a road. Go left along the road and right at the fork in 40 yards. Pass houses on the left, ignore the fork to the right, and pass a large farm building. Immediately take the waymarked path to the left and follow it for ¾ mile, with the River Beane on the left, to Stapleford.

Stapleford Church has a 12th century nave. Additions were made in the late 19th century, including an interesting and unusual tower.

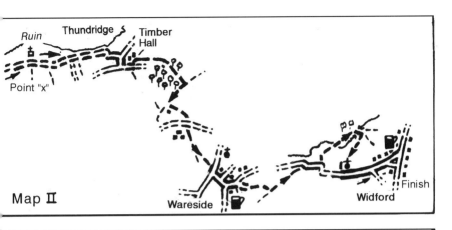

Map II

Ruin
Point "x"
Thundridge
Timber Hall
Wareside
Widford
Finish

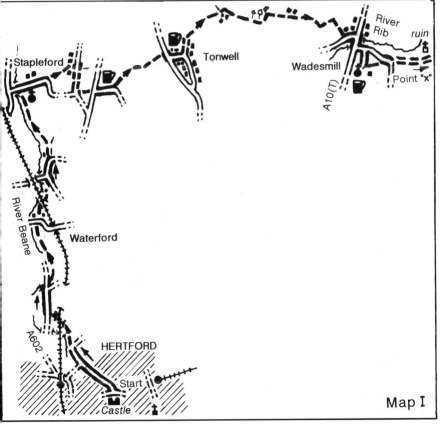

Map I

Stapleford
Tonwell
Wadesmill
River Rib
ruin
Point "x"
A10(T)
River Beane
Waterford
A602
HERTFORD
Start
Castle

Route map for Leg 11

Hertford, Parliament Square © Anthony Mackay

3. Pass to the left of the churchyard and turn right along the road. After about ¼ mile where the road swings right, take a footpath over a stile on the left. Cross the field diagonally to a stile in the far left hand corner. After crossing the stile, take the track to the right. On reaching a road, take the footpath on the left, crossing a field to reach a road at the Three Harts pub. Take the road continuing in the same direction as the path (signposted to Chapmore End). Where the road swings to the right, take the footpath to the left. This crosses between fields and then follows the edge of a field with a hedge on the right, to reach a main road.

4. Cross this with care and take the road ahead into Tonwell. Pass the Robin Hood & Little John pub and in 25 yards turn left along Temple Lane. Continue in the same direction along the track to farm buildings (Bengeo Temple). Pass to the left of the buildings following the waymarked path and immediately cross a stile on the right to follow a path along the back of the buildings, crossing a wooden footbridge, and continue ahead. Cross a stile and a ditch on a plank and go left along the track. At the bottom of the hill go straight ahead across a track and climb the hill through trees on a waymarked path, swinging left up steps to reach the top. Continue along the side of the field with a hedge on the left. The path swings left and then right, and in 30 yards goes through a gap in the hedge. Continue ahead with the wood on the left and in 50 yards go diagonally right across the field towards the farm buildings.

5. Pass to the right of the farm (Chelsing Farm), cross a track (waymarked on a post to the right), and continue straight ahead to the edge of the next

field. Follow the field edge with the hedge on the left. At the field corner, go straight on up a small rise, turn left for 15 yards, then right and go ahead past telegraph poles. Turn left at the end of the field (waymarked) and follow the top of the bank. At the next field, turn right and follow the path downhill into Wadesmill.

Wadesmill. The original church is now just a ruin ¹/₂ mile along our route. Just to the north of Wadesmill on the A10 is an obelisk (¹/₄ mile) to the memory of Thomas Clarkson who devoted his life to the abolition of slavery. He was born in 1760 and saw slavery abolished in the British Empire in 1834. The 'new' church in Thundridge is worth a visit.

6. At the road, turn left and proceed to the main road (A10). Turn right along the A10, cross over, and take the road to the left past the post office. Turn right up the hill and where the road turns right again proceed straight on for 10 yards and then take the footpath to the left (signposted Thundridge Old Church). Follow this path through two fences onto a metalled lane and continue to the right along the lane.

Thundridge standing on the route of the Roman Ermine Street, was the site of the first turnpike gate, set up in 1663. The walk passes the ruined tower marking the site of the Norman parish church. You can still see part of its Norman doorway-sadly vandalised.

7. Where it swings right, go straight on along the bridleway. Continue

Thundridge - The ruined church
© Nancy Scott

past the church ruin ignoring the footpath on the left, pass through a small swing gate, cross a concrete drive between trees, and swing left to the river. Follow the riverbank for about ¹/₂ mile and then turn right and continue on the path, uphill between hedges, to reach a road. Turn right along the road and in 100 yards where the road turns right turn left through white metal gates bearing the name Timber Hall. Proceed past the house, turn half left and continue past barns on the left. In 100 yards, passing a small wood on the right, go right into a field and follow the left hand edge of the field to the corner of a wood. Take a path into the wood and follow it, crossing a wooden bridge, to continue on track. Where this emerges onto a lane, turn left past cottages on the right (Legges Cottage), and proceed to a road.

8. Cross straight over to a stile and cross a second stile in about 50 yards. Continue with a wire fence on the left through a gate and then in 100 yards cross a stile on the right onto an obvious track. Continue in the same direction with a wire fence on the left and then a hedge on the right. At the corner of the hedge, turn half left and cross the field to the opposite corner (a path may be apparent or may have been temporarily ploughed out). The path leaves the field through a gap between tall trees and goes down steps to a road. Turn right and immediately left and follow the road downhill into Wareside.

9. At a T junction with a main road, turn left, pass a footpath sign on the right and take the clear track 10 yards further on the right. Follow this with a stream on the right, cross the stream on a wooden bridge, and continue round the right hand side of the next field to meet an old railway track. Turn left here and follow the track until it is blocked. Continue on a track forking right at this point and in 200 yards take a path to the left on to a road. Turn right along the road and where it turns to the right take a RUPP to the left. Follow this, crossing a bridge over a river (the Ash).

10. Proceed with a wood on the left. Cross a stile and follow the path to the right along the edge of the field with the river on the right. About half way along the field turn right and cross the river by a footbridge. Follow the hedge round to the left and cross a stile onto a track. Follow this track to the right and go up the hill towards the church, entering the churchyard by wooden steps. Looking back just before climbing the steps gives an excellent view of the valley. Go through the churchyard and follow the road to the left to reach the centre of Widford.

Widford has associations with Charles Lamb: he was a frequent visitor to his grandmother who lived there (see leg 12). Parts of the church are very old, and it boasts five wall paintings dating from the 14th century. There are good views of the Ash Valley from the church.

Researched and walked by Nancy and Michael Scott.

Leg 12: Widford to Bishop's Stortford

Length 11½ miles
Start Widford (village centre) **GR** 420159
Finish Bishop's Stortford Station **GR 492209**
Maps **PFM** 1074 & 1097 **LRM** 167
Public Transport Widford has a local bus service connecting with Hertford, Ware and Bishop's Stortford. Bishop's Stortford has bus and main line train services.   .
Pubs Much Hadham 3½ m, Perry Green 5 miles, Green Tye 6 miles, Thorley Street 9½ miles

The Route.   Basically the route starts along the Ash valley to Much Hadham. It then turns east over higher ground separating the Ash and Stort valleys past the hamlets of Perry Green, Green Tye and Thorley, now joined to Bishop's Stortford, then follows the Stort Valley to the centre of Bishop's Stortford.

We have now reached the arable country of east Hertfordshire, an area of small villages and large fields. This leg starts at Widford, a village on a hill beside the Ash valley. There used to be a railway station here on the now closed Buntingford to St Margaret's branch line. Cars can be parked in a lay-by just past the church on the Ware road. Charles Lamb, the early 19th century essayist (pen name Elia), spent his childhood summers at Blakesware, a large old country house near Widford, with his grandmother, the caretaker. The owners were often absent and Lamb acknowledged in his writings that the freedom to wander through the house and grounds, browse in the library and make trips in the surrounding countryside, helped shape his mental development and literary style. Blakesware has since been rebuilt.

The Walk

1. Start at the red telephone box in the village, just west of the Green Man pub. Take the signposted alley. Go left and right at the road crossing and follow the path into the country, downhill towards the river. At the bottom of the hill cross a stile into a green lane and turn right. Follow this path across a roadway and along the access road to a Three Valleys Water pumping station. Just before the gates turn left round the side of the compound, first on an enclosed path and then along the side of an arable field, to reach the B1004 road at a bridleway signpost. Take Bourne Lane opposite, and in 200 yards, turn left at a signpost 'PB Stansted Hill 1¼' at the HCC Hadham Towers site. Walk through the site bearing left to the bridleway. Keep on the lower path and follow the river valley north, for just over a mile, until you come to a road. Turn left and at the bend in 50 yards, keep ahead through a kissing gate across a meadow, rejoining the road by a ford.

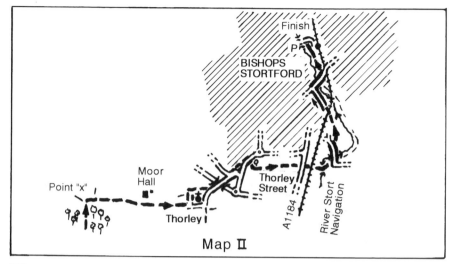

Map II

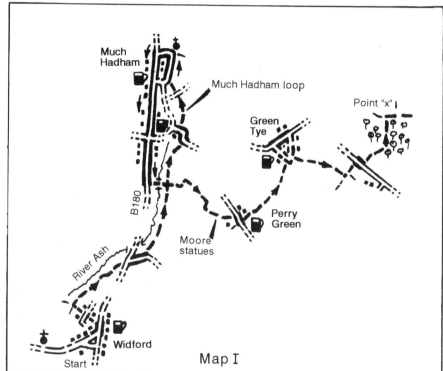

Map I

Route map for Leg 12

2. Don't cross the ford, turn sharp right along the road, and in 50 yards, at a signpost, climb a stile on the left. Cross a meadow to a kissing gate, turn slightly left and cross the next meadow, with the hill on your right, to another kissing gate. Cross the private drive, go through another gate, keep ahead, and cross a footbridge at the far end of the meadow to join a road by a house called 'Two Bridges'. Turn right and reach Much Hadham church in 200 yards.

The first Church on this site was in the 12th century but most of the present building is a jumble of styles from the 13th to 15th centuries. It is used by both Anglicans and Roman Catholics. The 20th century is represented by two gargoyles by the west door carved by Henry Moore. The 17th century mansion north of the church is The Palace, the former country house of the bishops of London. Inside the church it is recorded that the father of the first of the Tudors, Henry VII, was born in Much Hadham.

3. From the church go past a lamp-post in the churchyard and down an avenue of trees to the High Street and turn left.

As you go, admire the many and varied architectural styles of houses along the street. The village is one of the most beautiful in Hertfordshire. It is distinguished by the architectural quality and variety of its domestic buildings. It is outside the scope of this guide to describe the houses in detail but enjoy the architecture as you walk down the High Street. A camera or sketch book is handy here. There is a small museum in the old forge; check its opening times.

4. You will now walk about a mile along the High Street. Look out for open country on the left just beyond the derestriction sign. The path is on your left just before a white house and 100 yards before the Jolly Wagoners pub. Turn left on to it and cross the little River Ash and then a wooden bridge. You have now completed the Much Hadham loop, as you are crossing your original path into the village.

5. Cross a stile and climb the slope ahead, to the edge of the wood on your left, go round the wood and in 50 yards turn sharp right across the field with a telegraph pole ahead. Near the crest of the hill the path meets a T junction (old tree), turn right and in 100 yards turn left.

6. Before turning left notice the first of the Henry Moore statues across the field in the distance. Go past farm buildings on the left. Do not follow the track to the right but cross the stile by the gate on your left and keep straight ahead through the Henry Moore estate and admire his sculptures (it is a public footpath but the land around is private so please keep to the path). Go to the left of the house ahead and walk out to the road. At this point, on your right, notice the pub beyond the telephone box. Cross the road onto a small green and go through a gap to the left of Ash Tree Cottage and then turn left and follow the hedge.

The sculptor, Henry Moore, moved to Perry Green to escape the wartime bombing in London, and lived there until his death in 1988. The combination of

Yorkshire ancestry and the Hertfordshire countryside inspired his distinctive, powerful style. Several of his sculptures are visible from the route.

7. Keep Bucklers Hall Farm on your left and swing round a pond. Follow round the hedge on your left, with a large farm building also on your left, again keeping a northerly direction (sometimes the hedge becomes a ditch). In $1/4$ mile where the path enters a green lane, there is a path on your left. (Take this path if you want a pub in Green Tye, which is about $1/4$ mile). Return to this spot to continue the walk.

8. In 100 yards, just before the lane joins a residential road into the village, turn right at a footpath sign onto a field edge path. Keep ahead with bushes and then a ditch on the left, then cross the field to a foot-bridge. Cross it, keep ahead, and then turn left along a farm track to the road. Turn right along the road, and in 50 yards go left along an old aero-drome track towards a wood. Just before the wood turn left onto a track alongside, then through the wood. This area is the highest point of the walk between the Ash and Start valleys.

9. On leaving the wood, by an old concrete bunker, continue to a bridleway signpost, and turn right over a footbridge. The path soon becomes a farm track. In about $1/2$ mile, just past a barn, turn right along a concrete track and follow it to Thorley Church, $3/4$ mile away. The church is a mixture of styles from Norman to the 19th century. Just before the churchyard turn left onto a track and in a few yards go right through a kissing gate into the churchyard. Pass the north side of the church, go out through the lych-gate and walk down the road.

10. Cross over a new road, which is in a cutting, and keep ahead at a road junction. Just past a '40 mph' sign, when the road you are on turns right, keep ahead along a short disused stretch of road (this may disappear and become a wide grass verge!) and join another road. Just past a '30 mph' sign turn right through a gate beside a copse. Follow this field edge path round to the left and downhill, reaching the A1184 in $1/2$ mile. Cross it with care and take the path opposite. Cross the railway with great care, it's the main London - Cambridge line, and the river, and turn left along the towpath. The obvious way to reach Bishop's Stortford is to follow the towpath for $1 1/2$ miles past the Rushey Mead nature reserve, but this route goes into Essex where the county boundary follows the middle of the river.

11. So, to keep in Hertfordshire, stay on the towpath as far as the next road. Turn left along it and in 200 yards go right onto a short track opposite 'The Chase' house. Climb a stile on the left, cross a field corner and follow the field edge. In 200 yards at the next corner keep ahead and cross a stile into a lane. Turn right and **cross the railway with great care,** pass a small industrial estate and soon turn right along a main road.

Bishops Stortford   © Anthony Mackay

Cross the road, cross the river and turn left back on to the towpath. In a ¹/₄ mile, by a footbridge, turn right across the station car park. Buses stop near the Falcon pub, 100 yards north of the railway station. For the town centre keep on the towpath and turn left at the next road bridge.

Researched and walked by Chris Pagan

Leg 13: Bishop's Stortford to Hare Street

Length 12 miles
Start Bishop's Stortford Station **GR** 492209
Finish Hare Street **GR** 390295
Maps **PFM** 1073 & 1074 **LRM** 166 & 167
Public Transport Bishop's Stortford has trains and
buses. Hare Street has a limited local bus service
Pub Albury 6½ miles

The Route. We are now beginning to turn north as we walk the
penultimate leg of the Hertfordshire Way. Once we leave Bishop's
Stortford we are in a very rural part of the county, close to the borders of
Essex. It is a walk of open skies and wide views.

*Bishop's Stortford. Waytemore Castle, 'Wayte' meaning a place of ambush and
'more' a fen or marsh, is in the public gardens. It was the fortress of Bishop
Maurice of London, entrusted by the Conqueror to oversee the key position of the
ford over the River Stort. All that is left now is the mound on which the keep stood
and a few stones. Birthplace of Cecil Rhodes, son of the Rev F.W. Rhodes, Vicar
of St. Michael's. A museum depicting his life and work in South Africa is in South
Road. St. Michael's Church contains a memorial to the man who made the River
Stort navigable up to Bishop's Stortford. The canal was opened in 1769 by Sir
George Jackson who was the major shareholder and promoter, a friend of Captain
Cook who named Port Jackson in New South Wales and Point Jackson in New
Zealand after him. Sir George later changed his name to Duckett to fulfil the terms
of an inheritance from his second wife. Bishop's Stortford has a fine
pedestrianised shopping centre (market days Thursday and Saturday). There is a
small museum, well worth visiting, in the town Cemetery.*

The Walk

1. From the railway station and bus terminus walk towards the town over
the river bridge, turning right at the traffic lights to walk through the
semi-pedestrianised High Street. Turn left along Apton Road (first road
on the left opposite WH Smith) and later right along a path immediately
after Apton Centre, walking towards, then to the left of, St. Michael's
Church to reach Windhill. Go left up the hill and right at the top down
Bells Hill for a few yards before entering an alley on the left. Follow this
with first a school on your left and later a sports hall on your right. The
route briefly joins an asphalt path here and when this curves left continue
ahead making for a large gap in the hedge. Continue ahead through a
sports ground and on reaching the highest point walk towards the
fingerpost at the hedge corner.

2. Turn right, with the hedge on your left, and views to your right over
Bishop's Stortford. Exit the playing fields by a kissing gate and turn left
along the road and then right along a narrow path just before the entrance
to the sports ground. Follow the path as it bends right then left to enter

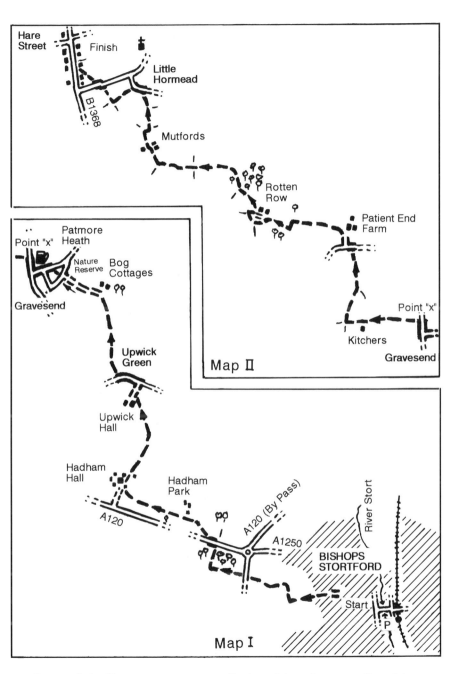

Route map for Leg 13

Based upon Ordnance Survey map with permission.
Crown copyright reserved

a small wood. Twenty yards into the wood turn right and follow a path through the wood to exit by the fence of the last house.

3. Our route continues alongside the fence on the left, crosses an estate road and later enters Squires Close. Cross another estate road. (Tesco supermarket is to the right for those needing sustenance) and later cross, with care, the busy estate link road. We now enter the open countryside and follow the right edge of the field heading for the woods in the distance. At the bottom corner go through a gap in the hedge and turn right making for an elevated section of the A120.

4. Go through the underpass and turn left along the original road, now used as access to a farm and cottages. At the end of the tarmac go over a stile into a field and aim half left making for the right side of the bungalow gardens. Continue on the same line to the corner of the field and then left alongside a gravel drive for a few yards before going over a stile and along a drive. On reaching the farm entrance and access from the road go straight on and in 20 yards go over a stile on the left. The path continues on the same line, parallel to the A120, making for a bridge on the right of a small wood. A second field is now crossed on the same line making for a gate on the far side between two hedges. Go half right across the next field to the right of the tennis courts in the far corner.

Hadham Hall   © Anthony Mackay

5. Then go through a gate and right along a drive to Hadham Hall through an arch (Pudding Stones here).

Hadham Hall is a Tudor building lately used as a school but now a housing development. The grounds were once parkland. Partly built in 1575 and owned by the ancestors of the Earls of Essex. The nearby church of Little Hadham will repay a visit with its fine setting of cottages and farm buildings.

Pudding Stone is composed of rounded pebbles stuck together with natural cement that has washed between them and hardened into solid rock. Rarely found outside Hertfordshire and Essex.

6. Proceed ahead later curving right and left, first with a pond on your right then with another on your left. On entering a corner of a field follow a gravel bridleway left (north) with views to the left over the Ash Valley and Albury Church. The bridleway later passes an old moated site surrounded by trees. Ignore a track coming in from the right but continue on the same northerly line of bridleway now grassy, later between hedges, passing Upwick Hall on your left and along a drive to the road.

7. Turn left and after 300 yards turn right along a road to Broome Farm with Pillar Box Cottage on your right. Where the drive swings left towards some buildings continue along the bridleway with a hedge on the left and follow this as it descends past a wood on the left and then uphill. After another gentle descent and ascent the track enters the edge of a small wood and then with a hedge on the right reaches an asphalt road. Cross the stile on the other side of the drive and walk 25 yards across the narrow corner of the field and over another stile to join a stony track (in practice it is easier to follow the drive right and left to avoid climbing two stiles). Follow the stony track as it goes gently downhill and then up to the houses surrounding Patmore Heath.

Patmore Heath is managed by Hertfordshire and Middlesex Trust for Nature Conservation. One of the best examples of an acid heathland in Hertfordshire on the Reading Beds (sand & gravel). The open grassland of the heath has gone over to scrub in recent years. Grazing by sheep has recently been started again to maintain areas of grassland. There are a number of ponds on the heath but with dry summers and the lowering of the water table through abstraction, these are often dry. Some of the flowers on the heath are found in few or no other places in the county.

8. Cross the heath ahead turning half left towards the end to reach the road, (there is a piece of pudding stone by the edge of the road). Turn left down the road to reach the Little Hadham/Furneax Pelham road and the Catherine Wheel pub.

9. Turn right along the road for 200 yards. Turn left immediately beyond the last property on the left, down a stony track and over the River Ash (often dry in summer). The way continues ahead to the right of a wood up the hill, passing a large house and grounds on the left, then right on a

cross track, later descending to a footbridge over a stream and uphill between fields to reach the road at Patient End.

10. Here turn left and immediately right onto a track to the farm. Where the track enters the farm keep left and follow the track between fields away from the farm buildings. The track swings gently left now with a hedge on the right. It later swings right (less clear now) still with the hedge on your right. At the field corner, near a wood, go over an earth bridge and left for 80 yards with a ditch on your left to a field corner. Here go right with the hedge and ditch on the left.

11. On reaching a pond and building at Rotten Row turn left alongside the fence, skirting the pond and gardens on the right, to reach a drive to a house. Cross the drive by a waymark, enter a field and turn right; Eighty-five yards later go through a gap into another field and return to the drive. Eighty yards beyond the house leave the drive again, turning left to cross a field (NW) to the distant corner of the wood.

12. Enter the wood and in 10 yards ignore the path on the left but swing gently right on a path just inside the wood, later scrub area, before heading across a field towards a hedge (aim for the corner). Now keep

Hare Street   © Anthony Mackay

this hedge on your left and walk until you meet another one at a right angle to yours. At this point go through a gap in **your** hedge (left) and follow the new hedge with it on your right. You cross another track and then when the hedge swings right continue ahead in the same direction, as your way descends across a huge field to finally reach a cross farm track. Here turn right to reach the farm building and left after passing a black barn.

13. Go right in front of the gardens of a house and later a large farmhouse and outbuildings and downhill on a crossfield path to reach a hedge at the bottom. Turn right for 100 yards and pass through a gap by some old gate posts to cross the corner of a very narrow field. Now climb up the hill ahead keeping the hedge on your right to reach the road at Little Hormead. Turn left along the road to reach the church.

Little Hormead Church has a Norman doorway with a rare 800 year old door and 12th century ironwork.

14. The footpath enters the churchyard and leaves by the back across a field to a grass track. This is often overgrown and difficult to follow so it is easier to go just beyond the church and turn left along the grass track as it skirts the north edge of the churchyard and then wends its way downhill through a gateway to reach a long narrow meadow. Turn right here and exit the meadow by a stile or gate at the road. Turn left over a bridge and in 100 yards turn right by a fingerpost to head diagonally across a field to the end of a row of houses. At the corner turn left to reach the road and then right into the village.

Hare Street. A rather scattered village with a good tea room and handsome houses of the 16th and 17th centuries with overhangs, such as the former Swan Inn. The brick Georgian Hare Street House has its own small chapel.

Researched and walked by Roy Wheeler.

Leg 14:   Hare Street to Royston

Length   11½ miles
Start   High Street by Hare Street garage **GR** 390295
Finish   The Cross Royston **GR** 356407
Maps   **PFM** 1026, 1049, 1050, 1073, 1074
      LRM 154, 166, 167
Public Transport   Royston has regular bus and train services
      with major centres. Hare Street has a limited local bus
      service.
Pubs   Great Hormead 1½ miles, Anstey 3¾ miles,
      Nuthampstead 5 miles, Barkway 7 miles,
      Reed 8½ miles.

The Route.   The final leg takes us back to Royston and in the later part
we descend the scarp that we climbed on our first walk but on a gentler
path.   But first we take our last look at the gentle rolling hills of
Hertfordshire and view a few more of its charming villages.

*Information on Royston can be seen at the beginning of Leg 1. Hare Street boasts
both a pub, The Beehive, and the Old Swan Tea Shop.*

The Walk
1. Start at the bus stop by Hare Street garage and take the footpath close
by beside a house called Timbers.   The footpath will take you to a
recreation ground, where you should aim for a bridge across the river,
although there may not be much water.   Shortly after crossing the bridge
the path forks.   Take the right hand path, which runs directly ahead in an
easterly direction to a stile.   Here cross into a meadow and you will
shortly come to two further stiles crossing a track.   After crossing both
stiles, you will see a large house on your right, Great Hormead Bury.

2. Look out for a stile on your right and cross this to go down the side of
the house to reach St Nicholas Church, Great Hormead. Walk through the
churchyard on a grass path, which will bring you out to the road at a gate.
Here cross the road to a track which is signposted as a RUPP.   Follow this
to a junction, where you turn left (north) and continue to follow the track
to a corner.   Here leave the track and resume your northerly direction by
following a footpath to a stile. Cross this into a meadow downhill to a
narrow path between a hedge/fence and down steps to the road at Great
Hormead.   *The Three Tuns Pub is a short distance down the road to
the left.*

3. To resume the walk, turn right along the road, then take the first road
on your left, just before a corner. Follow this road to immediately before
the entrance to Great Hormead Hall, where a footpath (left), follows a
hedge parallel to the road through the farm. This footpath leads to a stile.

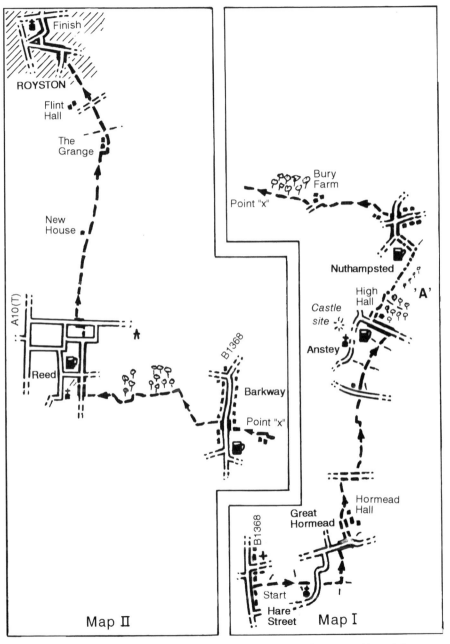

Route map for Leg 14

Based upon Ordnance Survey map with permission.
Crown copyright reserved

99

Cross the stile, cross a meadow to another stile, to join the track at the far side of the farm. Turn left on this track and follow it to a further stile at the road. On reaching the road, turn right (east) along the road for about ¼ mile to a footpath left, which enables you to resume your northerly direction. This crosses a field to a bridge.

4. Follow the right hand side of the field, beside a ditch, continuing northwards. This path becomes a good grass track and should be followed to the road at Daw's End. Cross the road, slightly right, to a footpath opposite. This crosses a field to a bridge, then downhill beside a hedge to a further bridge

If you wish to visit St George's Church at Anstey take the footpath going due west immediately before the second bridge. This church is dedicated to our patron saint, St George. There is a lock-up at the entrance to the church and an interesting moat behind it into which an American bomber, from the nearby airfield at Nuthampstead, crashed during the second world war. The plane was fully loaded with bombs and all 10 crew were killed. Fortunately for Anstey the bombs did not explode. The moat is all that remains of the castle but in the church are some medieval graffiti, which is more fitting to a bored soldier in the castle than a saint in the church. There is also an old AA sign giving mileages. Hare Street 2¼, Meesden 1¼ and London 34. The walk may be rejoined by continuing down the road past the Chequers pub (bus timetable on the side) to a well head. Take the footpath opposite and follow a grass path to a bridge. Do not cross it. Turn left to the road.

5. To continue the walk, cross the substantial bridge ahead, across a field, then continue straight ahead with a ditch on your left until the path turns right beside a ditch. Just beyond the corner turn about to go west to pass the other side of the hedge over a bridge. Turn right to the road. At the road turn left. Just beyond High Hall Farm, take a footpath right, signposted 'Lower Green 1¾'. On reaching a yard, pass through a fence on the left, then follow the fence. When the fence ends continue through the meadow to join a track beside the wood. Follow this track which runs along the outside of the wood. There are good views left.

At this point we are going onto a permissive path GR 410337 until 412346 (the Woodman pub see Sketch map A). Many rights of way 'disappeared' from maps during the war. We will be walking on a section of old runway which is not recorded on today's maps as a right of way but is a permissive path granted by the landowner.

6. Ignore a footpath through the wood on the right and continue along the track until it meets three concrete roads. Here follow the furthest left road. Just beyond where the trees by the middle road end and before a circular aerial array, take a concrete road left, which becomes a grass track. This conveniently comes out beside the Woodman pub at Nuthampstead. Two flag posts can be seen nearby. *By the Woodman is a memorial to 398 Bomb Group and there are pictures and other memorabilia inside. It*

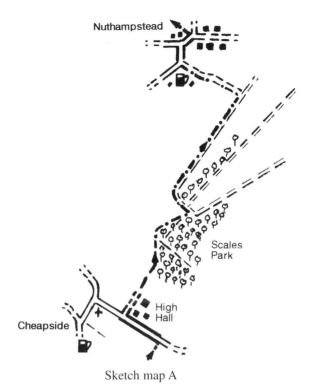

Sketch map A

may also be possible to purchase a map of the area as it was in the Second World War.

7. To resume the walk, turn right from the Woodman down the road signposted to Barley. Ignore the road bearing right which, although the road markings indicate it is a major route, is in fact a cul de sac. Immediately after passing this road take a footpath left over a stile. Follow the waymarks through two gates, then cross another stile. Go across a field then through a hedge/copse turning sharp left to follow this hedge (now on your left) for 50 yards before following a ditch west (two trees at start of ditch). After 300 yards leave ditch heading slightly left. Keep on a straight line (west) with Bell Farm to your left.

8. Our route crosses a bridge, then along a grass path to come out to the road at Bury Farm. Here cross a stile ahead, but slightly right, into a meadow. Cross a double stile. Turn half left and head for the far end of a large wood, which is on your right (at the time of writing there is a large white sign ahead of you). Cross a stile in the corner of the field. From the stile, the path runs along the south side of Earl's Wood mostly on a good grass track. On reaching a T junction, turn right along the track, which bears left almost immediately to resume your westward direction.

At a corner, where the track turns right, keep straight ahead along a foot-path to the road at Barkway. The Tally Ho pub is a short distance down the road to the left. Buses call at Townsend Close. To continue the walk, turn right down the road to a footpath left, opposite No. 93, signposted to Reed 1½ miles.

In the days of stage coaches, Barkway was a very busy place, being on the main road between London and Cambridge. Although none is open to the public, there are many interesting old houses in Barkway. No. 93 is a Wealden house dating from 15th Century. Continue down the High Street if you wish to see the milestone erected in 1725 by Dr. William Warren, Master of Trinity Hall, Cambridge. The finance came from bequests, by two Fellows of Trinity Hall named Mouse and Hare, made 150 years earlier for the upkeep of the highway. These milestones are measured from St Mary's University Church in Cambridge and the first milestone is at the side of Trumpington Road at the end of Brooklands Avenue.

9. To resume the walk take the footpath, which is fenced at both sides, to a stile. Cross this and resume your forward direction with a hedge on your right. Beyond the end of the hedge the path turns right across the middle of the field, across a bridge to a track directly opposite. Follow this north-west then west for æ mile. At a T junction turn right then resume your forward direction beside a line of single, tall trees. At a corner, a footpath goes directly forward to Reed Church. *(Follow this to visit the church).*

The village has a remarkable grid-like lay out which makes archeologists think that it was a Roman settlement for pensioned solders, though no Roman remains

Reed Church   © Bert Richardson

Bridleway from Reed to Royston   © David Allard

have been found in the area. There are many moated sites in the area probably from troubled times in the medieval world.

10. Otherwise turn right with the track to a stile into a meadow. Cross this and follow the direction of the waymark to a pumping station, where there is another stile. Cross this and turn right to the road to pass the Cabinet pub.

11. Continue down the road to a T junction. Cross the stile directly ahead by a pond to a further road. Here turn left for a short distance then right along a bridleway signposted Royston 2½ miles. The track can be seen ahead going north. At Hatchpen, where there are notices saying 'Farm vehicles crossing', ignore the concrete crossing track and on reaching the track beyond the second notice, turn left on the track and resume your forward direction, passing a large house on your left. When the track turns left, continue ahead. Also ignore the track turning off right. Continue your forward direction north, crossing a grass track and passing through a gate. On reaching the entrance to the Grange, look out for the word 'Footpath' (actually a bridleway) painted on a fence.

12. Go right up to this fence and follow the path, which will take you round the Grange and on northwards (ignore crossing path) up a hill and across a track, then downhill to the end of Grange Bottom. At the end of this road, turn right into Beldam Avenue, then left downhill. This is Barkway Road, which becomes Barkway Street. After joining Priory Lane (A10 one way system), follow the road left to the bus station. Cross

by the zebra crossing to the Chequers Hotel at the top of the High Street. The official end of the walk is at the Cross at the bottom of the High Street, where Royse Stone is.

Researched and walked by David Allard

You have now completed the 166 mile Hertfordshire Way

We welcome any suggestions that might improve the route or the guide book text: such as additional background information, sketches or photographs etc. These will be considered for a future edition. Please write to the address below.

FRIENDS OF THE HERTFORDSHIRE WAY

The organisation was set up to promote and develop this long distance route. We need new supporters to ensure that the long term future of the route is assured. We are looking for people who can fill one or more of the following needs! The first one is most important.

1. People who are too busy to give practical help but support us with their money and moral backing.

2. Supporters who can help in the field with such tasks as waymarking, checking an individual leg to make sure all is in order.

3. Helping to update the guidebook.

4. Joining the committee to help with organisational tasks and fund raising.

For more details of the Society send a stamped addressed envelope (22cm x 11cm, 8^1/$_2$"x 4^1/$_2$" or larger) to:

Friends of the Hertfordshire Way,
53 Green Drift,
ROYSTON, Hertfordshire
SG8 5BX